The Gospel Stories
of Jesus

Gospel Reflections for Year C

Luke

By Deacon Dick Folger

Watercolor sketches by the author

The Gospel Stories of Jesus
Copyright © 2003

By Deacon Dick Folger

Published by

2339 Davis Avenue
Hayward, CA 94545-1111, U.S.A.
510-887-5656
www.folgergraphics.com
E-mail: dickfolger@aol.com

Printed in the United States of America

Library of Congress Control Number 2002094888
ISBN 0-9715211-2-3

How others have used
The Gospel Stories of Jesus

J esus was a storyteller. And so we are all called to be storytellers for Jesus. In the closing words the Book of Matthew (28:19) we are commissioned: "Go then, to all peoples everywhere and make them my disciples!"

Sunday church bulletins are great opportunities for telling Gospel stories. Our bulletin had been static for years. The front page had a picture of the church and just listed the Mass schedules and various parish phone numbers. It was the same week after week.

In an effort to make the front page of the bulletin more readable, we began printing my paraphrase of the weekly Gospel story. We included an illustration and a short reflection. We sent the statistics to page two. People seemed to like the stories, so I kept writing and by the time we had printed the full three-year cycle, I had written 152 stories.

The Gospel Stories of Jesus were next published in Celebration, the worship resource of The National Catholic Reporter. This gave the stories a national audience and a much wider use.

Many churches began to print them in their Sunday bulletins. At a church in Baton Rouge, LA they even read one of the Gospel stories at Sunday Mass.

A Franciscan priest wrote to say he found the stories "extremely helpful for me as I prepare for my Sunday homily." Another reader said "I love to read them on Monday and walk with the story or image for the week."

A jail chaplain in California wrote to say, "I find them a wonderful way to share the Gospel story with the inmates in Saturday chapel."

Bible study groups have used the stories as "meeting starters" and youth ministers say the kids like to hear these "mini-movies" of the Gospels.

This book is copyrighted, but readers are welcome to reprint the individual stories in church bulletins or other materials as needed. No written permission is required, providing the following copyright reference appears:

© The Gospel Stories of Jesus by Deacon Dick Folger.

Deacon Dick Folger

Table of Contents Year C

The Sundays of Ordinary Time

The Sundays of Advent and the Christmas Season

Toward

the light...

The moonless night sky was sprinkled with silver stars. On the dark hillside a group of men were camped, circled around a cooking fire.

"How will we know?" Philip asked, fervently leaning forward, placing his hands on Jesus' arm. The disciples were enthralled as Jesus continued to tell them about their coming redemption. Like a prophet, he was revealing a vision of the future—a privileged glimpse at their own destiny.

Jesus' eyes reflected orange from the flickering campfire. His tolerant smile was filled with love for these followers who shared the moment with him. The words rushed to his lips.

"There will be signs in the sun, the moon and the stars. On the earth, nations will be in anguish, distraught at the roaring of the sea and the waves. Men will die of fright in anticipation of what is coming upon the earth. The powers in the heavens will be shaken." Jesus paused letting the images fill their minds.

No-one spoke as Jesus continued: "After that, men will see the Son of Man coming on a cloud with great power and glory. When these things begin to happen, stand up straight and raise your heads, for your ransom is near at hand."

Philip did not even blink as the answer to his question came so clearly. In his mind the sky was already ablaze with God's glory.

Peter unstopped the wineskin and felt the good burn as he swallowed some wine. Jesus noted this and continued, eyeing Peter as he spoke.

"Be on guard lest your spirits become bloated with indulgence and drunkenness and worldly cares. The great day will suddenly close in on you like a trap. The day I speak of will come upon all who dwell on the face of the earth, so be on the watch. Pray constantly for the strength to escape whatever is in prospect, and to stand secure before the Son of Man."

The last flames of the campfire collapsed and only the glow of embers remained. They all sat there together in the darkness. Philip was still fearfully clutching Jesus' arm. They sat in the silent starlight, dreaming the visions Jesus had revealed.

✝

The vision of Jesus, coming in a cloud of power and glory as the Son of Man, has always seemed like an event that the world would watch simultaneously. But it could just as well be an individual vision that each of us will truly see on that day which will suddenly close in on us like a trap. Those who have claimed near-death experience have universally spoken about moving toward the friendly light. As we begin a new church year on this first Sunday of Advent, let us pray constantly for the strength to escape whatever is in prospect so that we can stand secure before the Son of Man.

Second Sunday in Advent
Luke 3: 1-6

'Make ready
the way of the Lord...'

The air was cold and John was glad to see the red rim of the sun erupt over the dark hills beyond the Jordan. The slate gray waters of the river began to sparkle with brush strokes of color reflected from the morning sky.

From a Roman encampment higher up, near the road to Jericho, a lone sentinel looked out across the wilderness. Squinting into the golden light and long shadows, he did not see the tiny figure of John at the edge of the river. He could not know that the world was changing before his eyes. He could not see the presence of God pouring his Word into the heart of the lone man in the desert.

In distant Capri, sunrise was still an hour away. The semi-retired emperor of Rome, Tiberius Caesar, snored alone in his bed, freed from the worries of office. In Rome the unscrupulous Sejanus had everything under control. In Judea the Roman prefect, Pontius Pilate was in charge and he in turn watched Herod Antipas and his half-brother Philip who ruled the local lands and territories along the Jordan where John was to begin his preaching.

Even among the Jews there was control and order. The High Priest Caiaphas and his father Annas were beginning their new day, unaware that their world was soon to be shaken by the fulfillment of the great prophesy of Isaiah.

Drenched in a sunlight made brighter by God's presence within him, John the Baptist began to walk along the river's edge. He had become the herald's voice in the desert. He was filled to overflowing with enthusiasm and joy. John could not contain himself. He shouted into the empty sky: "Make ready the way of the Lord..."

☩

The world was busy with its own affairs, taking little note of the lone voice of John in the desert. The mighty emperor of Rome and the powerful rulers seemed to be safe and secure. But God took one small man wandering in the wilderness and gave him the voice to proclaim the coming of the Lord.

There's a message there for our time. Like the world, we may be too busy to hear the voices which proclaim the coming of Jesus into our lives. We may also be

too busy to realize that we are sometimes called to be the voice which cries out in the wilderness. Unless we choose to do so, we cannot realize those words of Isaiah: that "all mankind shall see the salvation of God."

Third Sunday of Advent
Luke 3: 10-18

"*...with the Holy Spirit and fire!*"

John plunged the young soldier down into the water. Falling backwards, the soldier's arms shot outward as he splashed down, disappearing in a foam of bubbles. John's strong biceps bulged as he supported the young man's weight, lifting him back to his feet. Water streamed down from both of them as they stood in the waist-deep river.

The crowd around them pressed closer to the bank. John waded toward them, already preaching again with fearsome authority and power. One frightened woman in the crowd backed away as he came toward her, his black hair and beard whipped in wild tangles. John's camel hair clothes made him seem like a wild animal as he stalked up the bank.

After John warned them about the fires of judgment they asked him what they should do.

"Whoever has two shirts must give one to the man who has none," John roared. "Whoever has food must share it!"

Some of the despised tax collectors and their bodyguards were watching the Baptist. "What should we do?" they called out. John turned to face them, the extra coins they had collected for themselves still heavy in their purses. "Don't collect more than is legal," John said flatly.

John walked up to the friends of the newly-baptized soldier and said to them: "Don't take money from anyone by force or accuse anyone falsely. Be content with your pay."

The crowd began to bow to John as he walked past them. Refusing their deference, he explained: "I baptize you with water, but someone is coming who is much greater than I am. I am not good enough even to untie his sandals. He will baptize you with the Holy Spirit and fire!"

They stood in silence, mystified and wondering who it was that John was announcing.

✟

    John's words still sting today. Many may not have offered their extra shirt to someone in need. Many may not have shared their extra food with those who have nothing to eat. These commandments from John are an initiation into Christianity. To prepare the way for the Lord, John exhorts God's people to sacrifice their own comfort in order to help someone else. It is the first requirement of Christian love. It is also the true Spirit of Christmas.

Fourth Sunday of Advent
Luke 1: 39-4

The Visitation

The caravan began to move out, following the South Road, heading for Jerusalem and the other cities in the region of Judea. It was a small caravan of pack animals, but with plenty of armed men they would be safe from any robbers that might overtake them in the hills of Samaria. Mary walked close behind the guard who had been paid to protect her.

From the top of the first hill Mary looked back, tears forming in her eyes. Her parents, Anne and Joachim were still waving from down below. Joseph, standing near-by was looking down and did not see her final wave.

As Anne watched her daughter Mary wave down to her, she was filled with the memory of her promise to the angel. After years of childlessness, the vision had come to Anne and told her that she would have a child. In joy, Anne promised to dedicate the child to God.

Now the same thing had happened to Anne's older sister Elizabeth. Her husband Zechariah had received a vision announcing the birth of a son. Elizabeth became pregnant at her advanced age and now, in her sixth month, needed help. Anne knew that she had to send Mary.

The slow caravan would take four days and three nights to reach the hill country near Jerusalem. There Mary would find the house of Zechariah and her cousin Elizabeth. Zechariah was a priest in the temple at Jerusalem and Mary looked forward to the visit. At night, camped along the road, she stared up at the stars and dreamed of the adventure she was living.

It was late afternoon when the caravan came into the village of Zechariah. Mary gathered her belongings and rushed off to find the house. Elizabeth was seated at a table, preparing the evening meal. Looking up from her peeling, she heard her young cousin, Mary calling hello from the open doorway. At that moment the child in Elizabeth's womb gave a mighty kick. With her heart overflowing with a rush of love, Elizabeth got to her feet and moved toward Mary, praising in a loud voice: "You are the most blessed of all women and blessed is the child you will bear."

✝

*If we were to gather all of the characters of this drama together, it would
include the four angels who appeared in turn to Zechariah, Anne, Joachim, and
then to Mary. It would include all the parents. And finally it would include the two
babes yet to be born: John and Jesus. But the most amazing of all these miracles is
the unfathomable reality that within Jesus there is the person of God himself. The
mighty creator of the universe and the master of all time has placed himself within
an unborn child.*

*These events are like a mystery box. When you open one you discover that it
contains another box. Inside that smaller box is another, and then another. And
finally, the smallest of these boxes is the mystery of Jesus. And within Him is the
greatest mystery of all.*

Christmas
John 1: 1-18

And the Word became Flesh.

John's white beard bobbed up and down as he chewed on his bread. The years had claimed most of his teeth and chewing was a chore. Still, his eyes looked merry as he enjoyed the food and the company around him. He washed his breakfast down with a cup of cool water. "Let's get started," he said.

Several scribes sitting at the table with him were there for a day of dictating and writing. John struggled to his feet and hobbled over to his seat by the window. The morning air was cool and scented with Spring blossoms. The harbor of Ephesus was in view from his hillside home. The scribes set up their writing materials and waited.

John gazed out the window and let his memory cross the decades to the years in Galilee when he walked with Jesus. He remembered it all except for the beginning. His piles of writings had accumulated. There were many books but he needed to find a place to begin and tie it all together into one life's work.

Papias, one of the scribes, encouraged John to start, "Tell us about the beginning?"

John remembered that first day as he and his brother James were packing up the fishing nets and Jesus had called from the shore, inviting them to follow him. But before that there were the stories of John the Baptist announcing the coming of Jesus. Before that there were the stories of Bethlehem and Magi from the East. But the Gospel began before those things. John began to speak and the scribes began to write down the words he spoke.

"In the beginning was the Word; the Word was in God's presence, and the word was God." John waited while they wrote. Through the morning John continued as the inspired words flowed from his lips. Then John came to the culmination of his realization as he said to the scribes:

"The Word became flesh and made his dwelling among us, and we have seen his glory; the glory of an only Son coming from the Father, filled with enduring love."

✞

The celebration of Jesus birth is the celebration of his principal teaching, love. Christmas fills us with that love as we gather as families, as we exchange tokens of our love with each other, but mostly as we feel the joy of God's love for us in all of that.

The Holy Family
Luke 2:41-52

Didn't you know?

The families who traveled down from Nazareth to attend the eight-day Passover feast in Jerusalem had already been gone from home for two weeks. Joseph was eager to get back to his unfinished work at the shop in Nazareth. He was also eager to end the first day of the long walk home.

"Only two more days, Joseph," one of his friends cracked as he watched the tired carpenter inspect his sore feet.

"If these feet last that long," Joseph replied, thinking this would be the last year that he would do this big trip to Jerusalem.

"Joseph!" Mary interrupted, her face filled with fear.

"What?"

" Jesus has disappeared," she said. "He's not with the caravan, I've looked everywhere."

"How can that be, I thought I saw him walking ahead with the other boys!" Joseph asked.

"He's gone," Mary declared.

After a moment Joseph rubbed his sore foot and sighed: "We'll have to go back. We'll return to Jerusalem in the morning."

This disaster was going cost them another three days; two walking and one trying to find their son. Twelve year old Jesus was in big trouble!

They worried, sleepless, through the long night imagining all the things that might have happened to Jesus. At first light they parted with the caravan. At the end of a long day they had covered the 30-mile distance. They spent that night with Mary's cousin Elizabeth, who was also dismayed to learn that Jesus was missing. The next morning they entered the city in search of their son. Joseph and Mary were both physically and emotionally drained when they finally discovered Jesus sitting happily in the Temple talking with the elders.

Mary's eyes searched Jesus' face. "Son, why have you done this to us. Your father and I have been terribly worried about you," she asked, her voice edged with disappointment and relief.

With his innocent eyes wide with surprise, Jesus answered his mom: "Why did you have to look for me? Didn't you know that I had to be in my Father's house?"

In a flash of light, Mary recalled it all: the night that the angel had spoken to her; her own words of submission and later the words of Elizabeth. Mary's memory filled with her child's miraculous birth—the shepherds, the star and the stable.

A shiver of fear crossed her face as she struggled to comprehend that this child before her was somehow God.

Joseph was about to scold Jesus, but he felt Mary's hand press against his, so he calmed himself and said: "Come, son, it's time to go home."

✟

Living every day with Jesus must have made it nearly impossible for Mary and Joseph to realize his divinity. The routine of their daily life smoothed off the edges of the reality that Jesus was the Promised One. Their memory was gradually buried under the softly falling snowflakes of time. The dream angel's announcements and the miraculous birth lay hidden under the quiet years. And now, suddenly, all was revealed again!

Today's Gospel reminds us that our faith may be softened by the routine years that have passed. The edges of our understanding may also have been rounded off. Today's Gospel gives us a reminder that Jesus is the Promised One. As God's children we are called to say to the world around us: "Don't you know that we must also be in our Father's house?"

The Epiphany of the Lord
Matthew 2: 1-12

The Epiphany
of the Lord

The palace guards opened the gates for the three Persian rulers. The kings walked briskly under the Roman arch and out into the streets of Jerusalem. Sunlight brightened their colorful robes as they paused to look back.

Above, on the portico, Herod Antipas looked down on them, raising his hand in silent farewell. Herod closed his hand leaving his forefinger extended as a silent warning not to forget his directions to gather information about this "newborn king." Gaspar, Melchior and Balthazar nodded their heads respectfully to their host. They would return soon to "report their findings to him." Herod, the Tetrarch of Galilee watched his guests walk in the direction of the Jaffa Gate.

Outside Jerusalem the kings mounted the waiting camels and headed toward the Bethlehem hills. In the darkness of night they would continue to follow the star that had brought them to this distant land. There they would see the prophecy that had already been fulfilled. They would be among the first to worship the newborn king. They would bring him gifts of gold, frankincense and myrrh to sustain the Holy Family in their flight to Egypt.

Later that night, the kings camped within sight of the stable where Jesus lay. As they slept atop their royal robes they were filled with a vivid dream. A beautiful angel appeared to them. Her bright eyes and luminous skin were lit with unearthly light. She smiled and spoke in a voice that was like the music of tinkling bells fluttering like leaves in a breeze. "Do not return to Herod," she said.

At sunrise, Gaspar, Melchior and Balthazar packed up and mounted their camels. Heading home toward Persia, they rode silently, remembering the vision of Jesus and the angel in their dreams.

The lower rim of the morning sun lifted off the hills to the east and warmed their faces as it climbed higher. After a time the kings reined their camels to a stop. Looking back, they saw Bethlehem's buildings were now only a tiny smudge of gold on the sunlit hillside. Beyond Bethlehem they could no longer see the lofty heights of distant Jerusalem.

✝

We are all like the wise men, the astrologers, the magi, the three kings. We seek to find the same thing. We search for the Newborn King in our own lives. We, too, follow the star, the light that beckons, the light that invites us to faith. We bring the gifts of our love, our time and our talent, presenting them to Jesus, the king of our lives. And, like Gaspar, Melchior and Balthazar, we must have the courage to turn our back on the Herods of our world, returning to our faith by any possible route.

The Baptism of the Lord
Luke 3: 15-16, 21-22

'You are my beloved son.'

John the Baptist stood in the waist-deep water of the Jordan River and smiled as Jesus sloshed through the shallower water and climbed up onto the riverbank. His cousin's soggy tunic hung heavily as it shed the cold water. No sunlight was coming through the clouds and Jesus shrugged his shoulders against the chill.

Others who had been baptized were kneeling in prayer. Jesus moved toward them. He dropped to his knees, his eyes closed and his face relaxed.

At a greater distance and higher up on the bank the crowds stood, watching and wondering. Some were there to see for themselves this baptizer who might be the long-awaited Messiah. Others who had been there before had decided to be baptized and were returning to seek repentance and new cleanliness. A few were gentiles converting to Judaism.

From the river John shouted to everyone, "I am baptizing you in water, but there is one to come who is mightier than I." John swung his gaze to Jesus, kneeling with the others. Continuing to look directly at Jesus he said, "I am not fit to loosen his sandal strap. He will baptize you in the Holy Spirit and in fire."

Some of the people in the crowd were looking at the newly baptized Jesus when his white tunic burst to light. A break in the clouds allowed a thin shaft of sunlight to stream down, bathing Jesus in its golden light. The beam intensified and the light grew whiter. Inside the beam even whiter wings formed. A dove with outstretched wings seemed to float down in the light of the beam. When the dove drew close its wings began to slowly flap and a roaring whirlwind formed. Peals of thunder tumbled out of the mountains. Above the noise of the wind there was a smiling voice that spoke like a whisper in the ear. It said, "You are my beloved Son. On you my favor rests."

The people on the hillside stopped talking among themselves. Those newly baptized who were praying near Jesus got to their feet. John the Baptist's arms dropped to his side. Everyone stood there in awe, transfixed by the event. Time stopped. It may have seemed like a long time or it might have only been a moment, it didn't matter.

Jesus was still kneeling when the wind pushed the clouds together and shut off the shaft of sunlight. With the light snuffed out, the grey overcast sopped up the shadows. The whirlwind went racing up the eastern riverbank and disappeared over the

crest. The loud wind began to still itself, dissolving into whispering zephyrs that softly caressed everyone's faces. The white dove was gone. Only clouds filled the empty
gray sky.

✝

*When Jesus went to the Jordan to present himself to John for baptism he was
beginning his public ministry. In the rite of baptism today the celebrant calls it "a
new beginning of goodness." Each morning of our life we are called to return to
our own baptism. To pray that each new day of our lives will be a new beginning of
goodness.*

The Lenten Season

Bread, glory and angels

Jesus knew he was not having a dream. The wind was real, blowing hard enough to make him lose his balance. From the highest parapet of the Great Temple wall Jesus looked out across the deep chasm of the Kidron Valley far below. Beyond the valley were the dim yellow firelights on the western slope of the Mount of Olives, cloaked with the black night sky.

Satan's evil presence urged Jesus closer to the edge. He smiled, raising his eyebrows in mock fear as he peered over the wall to the jagged rubble far below. He started to put his hand on Jesus' back as if to give a fatherly assurance, but Jesus moved away. Satan's smile dimmed briefly.

Seven weeks alone in the wilderness had taken a heavy toll on Jesus. He was gaunt from lack of food. His parched skin was ashen with the desert's dust and his disheveled hair tangled down onto the shoulders of his dirty robe.

Looking fresh and assured, Satan flashed his big smile again.

"If you are the Son of God..." Satan oozed, as if such an idea was preposterous.

Jesus teetered on the parapet as the wind swept up the wall and over to top.

Satan continued, warming to his little game: "...if you are the Son of God then throw yourself down from here."

Jesus looked down at Satan's finely chiseled face and his sneering smile. Their eyes locked and the Devil wet his lips and excitedly began nodding his head in encouragement for Jesus to jump!

Jesus glanced down the vertical wall to the rocks and the rubble below. The height made his legs feel wobbly. He wished for something to grab onto, but there was only the sturdy staff of his faith.

With his final taunt, Satan pressed so close that Jesus could smell his breath as he quoted from the 91st Psalm, he said: "Scripture has it that He will bid his angels to watch over you. With their hands they will support you that you may never stumble on a stone." Satan's eyes danced merrily as he pretended to scan the heavens for the arrival of the angels that would catch Jesus before he fell to the rocks below.

Like startled birds, a flurry of thoughts raced across Jesus' mind. His tempter had only quoted part of the psalm, leaving out the words that explained God's protection was from things that befell his servants, and not from things that people might do

themselves.

The night wind suddenly stopped. Jesus calmly stepped down from the ledge, advancing. Satan stepped back. His smile vanished and his face was dark with impending defeat.

From the depths of his exhaustion Jesus felt a new power surge up in him as he remembered the words from the Torah. The story in the Book of Deuteronomy told how the Israelites had tested God at Massah.

With a strong voice Jesus banished his tempter. "Scripture also says that 'you shall not put the Lord your God to the test.'"

Jesus turned and began to make his way down the steps, leaving Satan alone on the ledge. The wind began to blow again. A gentle peace seemed to warm him as Jesus began the long walk to Galilee.

✝

Lent's arrival brings memory of the many times we have been tempted. We may have also been blinded by desire for material things, for power or position. Some may have tested God, making selfish demands. In this Gospel Jesus shows us by his action how we can overcome our temptation. Lent gives us 40 days to practice this as we begin our annual pilgrimage to Passion, Resurrection and Glory.

Second Sunday in Lent
Luke 9: 28b-36

Once upon a mountaintop

Peter was sleeping on his back and the noise of his own snoring awoke him with a start. Spluttering, he cleared his throat and opened his eyes. It was night.

Rolling himself onto his side, Peter sat upright, smacking the dry taste in his mouth. For a moment he did not know where he was, but looking around, Peter remembered he was on the mountaintop.

Earlier, in the afternoon, Jesus had brought Peter, James and John up the mountain to pray with him. Peter had been exhausted from the long, steady climb, and once he'd begun to pray, he must have dozed off.

In the starlight, Peter found James and his brother John sleeping nearby, curled up like pale crescent moons, wrapped in their white robes. Peter looked around for Jesus and did not see him. Alarmed, he got to his feet. Then Peter saw the strange, billowing light further up the mountain.

At the summit, enclosed in a brightening cloud of light, Jesus was standing with two men. Peter scrambled in the dark to wake the brothers. Unable to speak, Peter shook their shoulders, rousing them to their feet.

Peter, James and John cautiously climbed higher up the dark mountain to where the now dazzling figures were standing. It was a vision that no one had ever seen!

Moses was now the burning bush, swathed in light upon the mountain. Elijah, the great prophet, who 900 years before had stood on a mountain to defend Yahweh against false prophets. He now stood again, present with "God's Messiah."

The holy light grew even brighter as the disciples moved toward it. It was an experience they could not explain to anyone. Overwhelmed by the vision, they were frozen in silence, but their hearts were bursting with the joy blazing before them.

✝

As we move into the second week of Lent we find the image of Jesus absent in our barren church. We long for the reassuring vision of the Resurrected Christ bursting forth into our midst. But like the disciples who were privileged to be with Jesus at the mountain-top Transfiguration, we too have seen him in his glory and we too must follow that vision in our hearts and minds until the fire of his presence returns during our Easter vigil.

Third Sunday in Lent
John 4: 5-42

The Fig Tree

J esus pulled a ripe fig from the tree and dropped it into the open palm of Peter's hand. He smiled and then walked away. The fisherman broke the fig open and began to taste the soft fruit inside.

It had been another of Jesus' great teachings. Andrew sat on a big rock and watched his brother chew on the fig. "Do you understand what he meant?" he asked.

Peter nodded and continued to chew. Andrew was eager to share his own understanding, "It's about the soil. The soil must be prepared. If it's fertilized the tree will bear fruit."

"I know that," Peter replied, wiping his mouth with the sleeve of his robe.

"But think of it this way," Andrew went on. "If you and I were fig trees, what would we need to bear fruit?"

Peter snapped back. "You tell me."

"We'd need food and water. The soil is like God's presence around our roots. It's from the soil that we draw our ability to bear fruit. The soil is what nurtures us. God's love is what waters us. It's God's way of caring for us."

Peter stopped eating. "Yes, but in the story Jesus told us the tree was barren for three years!"

"But the gardener never gave up and took care of it. From God's mercy the tree was given another year to produce," Andrew finished.

Peter went over and pulled another fig off the tree and broke it open. "Brother, let me tell you this. I think the story teaches us something else. It's this. To produce fruit we need to prepare ourselves first. We have to dig our own soil and water it today. If we wait it will be too late for us. If we keep putting everything off until tomorrow, what happens if you die tonight?"

Andrew considered his brother's ideas and did not answer.

Simon did. "You both fail to remember the teaching that the fruit of a tree may not be eaten during the first three years," Simon said. "In the fourth year the fruit is sacred to the Lord. Only in the fifth year may you eat of it. I think Jesus' story tells us that we are in the fourth year and that we are sacred to the Lord and that when the fifth year comes we will bear great fruit."

It was getting late and the figs weren't filling the hunger in Peter's stomach.

"Let's head back," he said. The three men hurried after the others who had already begun to walk down to the main road and on to the town. Jesus, walking alone, was well-ahead of everyone.

The gold of the sunset colored their white robes, contrasting them against the darkening blue of the lake beyond.

✠

The Gospel parable is an invitation to ask ourselves if we are barren fig trees. Do we need to repent and make the changes in our lives that will enable us to be fruitful. We do not know when our day or hour will come. If we wait too long it will be too late. But, God's mercy is upon us if we choose to receive it. There is still hope!

Fourth Sunday in Lent
Luke 15: 1-3, 11-32

The Prodigal Son

The group of Pharisees and scribes came pouring out of the synagogue together. They walked briskly, holding their heads high, aloof and preoccupied with the important matters of the day.

One of the Pharisees, splendid in his white robe, glanced to the side seeing Jesus and the crowd that had gathered around him. He put his hand on the arm of the scribe next to him, slowing him to stop and look. The others gathered around.

"See," the Pharisee said, turning his face to all of them, "this man Jesus welcomes sinners and eats with them."

The others murmured their agreement, confirming their worry that Jesus was dangerous. As protectors of the Jewish tradition, the law and the Torah, the Pharisees needed to denounce Jesus.

Because they could read and write, the scribes had prestige and power since they served those in authority, the Pharisees, rulers, rabbis and merchants. They kept the journals and records and this gave them power because they had information.

Jesus heard their condemnation of him and was reminded of the story about a father with two sons. The younger son took his inheritance and left the family. The older son faithfully stayed with his father and worked the family farm. The father grieved for his young son hoping he would one day return.

Jesus saw how the Pharisees were like the older brother. These men of authority were the ones who stayed with the tradition and the law. They were resentful of anyone who did not do the same.

Jesus then looked around him at the eager faces of the poor, the tax collectors, the sinners. They were the outcasts. They were the ones who were like the younger brother. They had used up their inheritances and were now returning, hoping to find redemption and forgiveness. They wanted to hear Jesus preach.

Jesus realized he was the Father, the one who could forgive, the one who would be joyous at the resurrection of his youngest son.

The story would be a good lesson for all to hear, especially the smug Pharisees and their scribes who needed to leave their rules long enough to know that to forgive is to love. It would be a good story for the tax collectors and sinners to learn that to love is to forgive.

Jesus stood so that the crowd around him could better hear his words. He opened his arms to them all in a gesture of welcome and affection. His bright smile captivated them.

When they fell silent Jesus began to tell the story, "A man had two sons..."

As we listen to the familiar parable of the Prodigal Son perhaps we can find ourselves in each of the characters. Sometimes we can be the resentful Older brother. Sometimes we can be the loving and welcoming Father. Sometimes we are the "Prodigal", demanding our inheritance so that we can go and indulge ourselves. Maybe we've done that already. But only as Prodigal Sons and Daughters, when we return empty-handed and penitent to ask God for forgiveness, do we really learn the wonder of our Heavenly Father. That he loves us so is beyond our understanding.

Fifth Sunday of Lent
John 8: 1-11

"Nor do I condemn you..."

It was still dark when Jesus opened his eyes. He threw back his covers and sat upright for a moment. He took a deep breath and rubbed his face with his fingers. Jesus rolled his bedding into a tight cylinder and placed it out of the way on the shelf above the mat. He quietly made his way to the cooking area and dipped a cup of water from the crock on the countertop. In the stillness he could hear the breathing of the others. They could catch up with him later.

The chill, early morning air nipped at the back of his neck as he headed out of the house and along the roadway to Jerusalem. Jesus pulled his robe higher around his neck to keep the cold at bay. The road led to the western slope of the Mount of Olives. Jesus paused at an overlook from which he could see the great city of Jerusalem sleeping in the darkness across the Kidron Valley.

The sun was just brimming over the horizon when he reached the Great Temple. Climbing the steps he gazed up at the huge stone columns that marked the entrance. Taking a seat on a ledge forming the Royal Portico, Jesus continued his morning reflections. Except for the slow moving sentinels behind the wall turrets, Jesus had the courtyard to himself. The sun warmed him and the solitude and silence soothed him.

By mid-morning the scene had changed. The sellers had moved in, setting up their open-air stalls. Some of the courtyard regulars were already in place, taking their favorite people-watching positions. Jesus moved down among them, then descended the steps, pausing at the edge of the unpaved lower yard. A few followers from yesterday were beginning to encircle Jesus, waiting to hear him speak again.

Suddenly, a noisy mob came forward. Jesus recognized some of them as the same scribes and Pharisees who had also come to him the day before. They were taunting a woman whose tear-streaked face was weary with exhaustion and fear.

Hoping to trick him, one of the Pharisees called out to Jesus: "This woman has been caught in the act of adultery. In the law, Moses ordered such women to be stoned. What do you have to say about this case?"

Jesus said nothing. He rose slowly from his seat and took a few steps toward them. Crouching down he began to make tracings on the ground with his finger. The crowd tightened around him as other scribes and Pharisees echoed the challenge. "Yes. Tell us. What do you say about this?"

Jesus rose, squaring off against his clamoring adversaries. With the sweep of his eyes and his pointing finger he shouted back: "Let the man among you who has no sin be the first to cast a stone at her."

Jesus let his words explode against them and returned to silently writing on the ground.

After a time Jesus stopped writing and looked up. Only the woman remained, standing alone, her face buried in her hands, her shoulders shuddering with her soft sobs.

"Woman, where did they all disappear to? Has no one condemned you?" Jesus asked.

"No one, sir," she answered.

Jesus caressed her with a smile.

"Nor do I condemn you," he said. "You may go. But from now on, avoid this sin."

✝

In a world of quick media judgment it is easy to condemn first and ask questions later. Jesus' brilliant response, asking those without sin to cast the first stone, leaps from the Gospel pages into our own lives. During Lent we focus on our need to be without sin and to seek reconciliation for those sins we have committed. We are incredibly blessed that God loves us and says also to us: "Nor do I condemn you."

Passion Sunday
Luke 23: 1-49

"Crucify him!"

The noise of the crowd's shouting gushed through Jerusalem's narrow streets like floodwaters on the rampage. The sound of angry voices leaped over walls and around corners, spilling into the leather shop of Kalim Ephras. He was intently cutting a strip of leather when the noise startled him. He fearfully looked up from his work then angrily back down as he realized he had gone crooked. The leather strip was now ruined!

Kalim tried to calm himself and put his knife aside. He went out into the street, walking in the direction of the shouting.

A mob of people was gathering in the courtyard of the Antonia Fortress. Guards, high up on the turrets of the outer wall, glared down as Kalim passed under the open archway. Colonnades, like stone sentinels, framed the yard. Higher up, on a balcony, stood the great Pontius Pilate himself. Like his guards, the Roman Procurator of Judea glared down at these Jews with nothing better to do than come for the show.

"Who's he?" Kalim asked the man standing next to him.

"The bloody one in the red robe is called Jesus," he replied. "The other is old Barabbas."

Wise to the ways of appeasing the crowds, Pilate was not going to reason again on behalf of Jesus. He would send him to the cross and that would be the end of this unpleasant problem.

The crowd began to roar again. "Crucify him, crucify him." They continued in a rhythmic chant and Kalim joined his own voice in the fun. "Cru-ci-fy him, cru-ci-fy him..."

For a long moment Kalim thought that the bloody man in the red robe was looking at him. The tired eyes of Jesus seemed to have focused directly on Kalim, as he stood there in the midst of the shouting crowd. There was a terrible sadness in those eyes.

Kalim felt a shiver of fear race through him. He quickly turned away and started back to his untended shop. At the fortress archway he glanced back, but Pilate's balcony was deserted. Kalim hurried back to his shop. He would be more careful when he tried again to cut his leather strips.

As he worked he couldn't forget those haunting, sorrowful eyes that had somehow seemed to look right at him.

Kalim picked up his knife and carefully began to slice through the leather. There

was much to do and he needed to finish before Shabbat began at sunset.

Kalim only paused briefly to listen when later in the morning he heard the crowds shouting again down on the Via Dolorosa. "It's probably the procession for that bloody man Jesus," he thought, imagining the scene as they led him out to Golgotha.

✟

We may sometimes join the crowds of our day who call out for the crucifixion of Jesus. We may "crucify him" with our sins. We may "crucify him" with indifference as we love this world more than we love him. We may "crucify him" when we join Peter, denying that we even "know" the man.

Easter Season through the Sundays of the Lord

Easter Sunday
Luke 24: 1-12

Alleluia!

Peter's fingertips fluttered nervously as he reached out to touch the folded white cloth. His hand slowly descended, like a bird with outstretched wings, floating down to land. Gently his thick-fingered hand clutched at the burial cloth which had covered Jesus' face.

Peter's heart pounded as he knelt with John there in the dim light of the empty tomb. Other burial wrappings lay on the ground beside the stone bench where Jesus' body had been laid.

As his hand rested on the cloth Peter's senses grew sharper. He could feel the cold air of the tomb searching the back of his neck. The chill air smelled dank, like wet soil and decaying wood with traces of something sweet. Quiet hung on the air like a muffling fog. Only the sound of their breathing could be heard.

In the stillness Peter tried to swallow the lump in his throat, but it was forced back up by his anxious heart. Peter stared at the bench for a long time, finally looking over at John who was still kneeling beside him. John's eyes were frozen in wonder.

Their minds raced for answers. Maybe some group broke into the tomb to steal Jesus' body? But the guards had been outside... What was it that the women said back at the house? Something about remembering what Jesus had told them while they were in Galilee—that Jesus said he would be raised up on the third day.

Peter suddenly realized this was the third day; everything Jesus had told them was now coming true.

His hand, still resting on the burial cloth, made Peter feel connected to Jesus. His fingertips probed the cloth, trying to feel his friend's face below the shroud. Perhaps if he closed his eyes Jesus would be there. Peter suddenly felt the Teacher's presence behind him and almost turned to look. A curious joy surged by, and he knew Jesus had risen from the dead.

"He has risen," Peter declared, announcing the revelation to John. A joyous laugh welled up within Peter and came out as a helpless sob.

John looked into Peter's teary eyes. They glistened in the light from the tomb's entrance. Peter struggled to get to his feet. "Come, John. Jesus is out there. Let's hurry and tell the great news to the others."

They started to climb out into the light of the morning when Peter stopped short. He looked back at the folded cloth still lying on the bench. Jesus had left it there for him to take. Peter gently gathered it up in his burly hands. Holding it like a fragile bird, he clasped the shroud to his chest and stepped out into the glaring morning sunlight.

"Jesus is risen," Peter shouted, "Jesus is risen!"

Alleluia! Alleluia! Alleluia!

2nd Sunday of Easter
John 20: 19-31

Peace be with you!

Under cover of darkness the disciples found their way back to the room where Jesus had shared his last supper with them. The horror of Jesus' crucifixion stalked their minds and filled them with fear. If caught, they would be the next ones to hang upon a cross. There was no one they could trust except themselves. The disciples huddled together on this final night in Jerusalem.

They had locked the door of the dimly lit room and reeled under the impact of the memory of what had happened. Jesus had been captured, tortured and crucified. It was unbelievable, but now he was dead. Their years together were over. The dream was ended.

And worse, they too were in danger! The authorities wouldn't stop with Jesus alone. They wanted everyone who was his follower.

In their fear, the disciples found themselves talking over what had become of Jesus' body. The women had seen something. Mary Magdalen said she had spoken with Jesus. Peter had seen the burial wrappings himself and knew that Jesus had risen from the dead, just like Lazarus!

The firelight from the lamps danced shadows against the walls of the room. At daybreak they would slip out separately and make their way back to Galilee. There they would rejoin their families and try to pick up the pieces of the life they had left behind.

Instantly a sense of presence made the room grow silent and the disciples froze in wonder. From a distance the faint sound of breathing soon became a loud roar of rushing wind. As the noise filled their ears an intense white light flooded their eyes. Some of the disciples scrambled away, backing against the walls.

When the wind and light stopped Jesus was there, standing in their midst. His face beamed love. Seeing their terror he raised his hands over them and calmed them, saying: "Peace be with you."

☦

Many of us still hide behind the locked doors of our hearts. We are hiding from God. We turn up the volume on our radios and televisions so that we don't have to listen to him calling for us. If we don't hear we won't have to change and let him

42

into our hearts and lives. We hide from the challenge to really live our Christian
life. We leave undone the things that we might do if we were not afraid of being
identified as one of the followers of Jesus.

May we pray for the courage that would allow us to hear the rushing wind and
see the gentle light of his presence—and then to truly know the meaning of his
words: "Peace be with you."

Breakfast in Galilee

P eter was half asleep, lulled by the gentle rise and fall of his boat as it floated upon the quiet water. The first warmth of the new day danced on beams of golden light, flashing across the great Sea of Galilee from the far eastern shore. Eager for the sun's warmth, the six other men in Peter's sturdy boat turned in their seats to bathe their faces in the light.

The nets were all down but there were no fish, despite Peter's claims to the contrary. They drifted closer to the shore on the familiar water's of Peter's "spot" near Tiberias. After a full night of raising and lowering the nets, they were beyond despair.

"Let's go," Nathanael said.

Thomas added his frustration, "This lake's fished out. We might as well go home."

Peter eyed the protesters grimly.

The morning silence was broken by the sound of someone yelling from across the water. Peter scanned the shore to find the noisemaker. A lone man was standing on the beach. He cupped his hands to his mouth and called out again: "Haven't you caught anything?"

Thomas, hoping to use this insult to convince Peter to give up and head back to Capernaum, called back loudly, "Not a thing." He made a quick glance to see Peter's reaction. The big fisherman was scowling back at him.

"Put the nets down on the starboard side," the man on the shore commanded. Peter got to his feet. He was about ready to silence this challenge to his authority when the idea of changing the net to the other side made sense. "Let's try that," Peter said. The men quickly hauled the empty net into the boat and payed it out on the starboard side. Suddenly the lines securing the net to the boat grew taut. The water rippled about the boat as the force in the net seemed to tow it shoreward.

"Haul in!" Peter roared.

All hands began to pull on the net but it would not come up. It was either seriously snagged on something or it was seriously full of fish. Because the boat was moving they realized it had to be fish, lots of fish! Their faces relaxed and broke into smiles.

The surface of the water encircled by the net was seething with fish. Amazed,

John stopped hauling on the net and looked shoreward at the man standing there. A thrill of recognition surged through John and he heard himself cry out: "It is the Lord!"

In one unhesitating move, Peter saw the fish brimming in the net, looked ashore at the Lord, pulled on his tunic, dove over the side and began swimming jubilantly toward the shore.

✟

How many times has the Lord appeared on the shore of your life? Do you remember the times when he called out to you? Did he ask "...have you caught nothing?" and have you heard him suggest that you "...lower your nets on the other side?" Jesus promised us, "I am with you." When we receive Eucharist he is "in" us. He is the gentle shepherd, guiding us in the right paths. But first, like Peter jumping from his boat, we must hear his voice and respond to it.

Fourth Sunday of Easter
John 10: 27-30

Like shepherds they came...

The words of Jesus sounded in the sea winds which filled Paul's ears as he stood at the ship's rail. The big boat was bashing steadily toward the port of Perga, driven on the fresh wind which seemed to be whispering the sayings of Jesus to Paul. Like running sheep, white foam gushed from the crashing waves being cleaved by the boat's bow. The sheep image triggered Paul's memory of one of Jesus sayings: "My sheep hear my voice. I know them, and they follow me."

Ahead, the southern coast of Pamphylia was waiting in the afternoon sun. Paul imagined himself as a shepherd coming into this region to call the Christian flock together.

As they neared the land, Paul recalled another saying of Jesus: "No one shall snatch them out of my hand." Beyond the bright, green trees and the white buildings Paul could see the tall, lavender mountains which he and Barnabas would soon be climbing. They would take the message of Jesus beyond those rugged peaks and claim new followers. With the strength of his preaching and the help of Barnabas they would build strong faith communities along the way. These would be communities of Christians that would endure. And no one would snatch these new believers away from them!

Paul's journey from Antioch had first taken him to the island of Cyprus and then northerly across 200 miles of boisterous open sea. Now the water was flat as the ship lowered sails and slowly ghosted into the harbor. Paul and Barnabas watched as the sailors heaved lines ashore, set out fore and aft anchors and warped the boat snug to the stone quay. The boat crew rigged a narrow wooden gangplank from the deck to the quay. Paul hoisted his bag of belongings and carefully walked the plank, arriving ashore with relief. After five days at sea his legs stiffened to meet the next sea swell, but the ground didn't rise and he almost stumbled.

"Solid land," Barnabas grinned as they swaggered up the pathway toward Perga. It was the start of a great adventure and the beginning of Paul's first mission. Ahead was a hike of 100 miles to cross the mountains of Pisidia.

Paul felt excitement course through him. He was filled with the Holy Spirit and eager to preach the Gospel of Jesus Christ—to tell the story of the resurrection 13 years ago; to deliver and plant the seeds of Christianity in the hearts of these distant

flocks of Jews and gentiles—Greeks and Romans.

Because of the success of Barnabas and Paul the strict Jews would soon expel them from one of the towns. But this rejection would not stop them—it only refueled their fervor.

Paul smiled to himself as the confirming words of Jesus whispered again in his mind: "My sheep hear my voice. I know them, and they follow me."

Those with faith hear the Shepherd's voice, know the truth and follow him.
They are secure in the knowledge that no-one can snatch this truth away from them.

Fifth Sunday of Easter
John 13: 31-33, 34-35

'I Love You!'

Jerusalem was getting noisy. It was the day before the Passover Festival and the city was crowded with pilgrims. There was an excitement in the air. Food vendors and wine merchants were cashing in on the annual boom in their business.

The sounds of good spirits, laughter and shouting, fueled by plentiful wine, filled the streets. Noise from the crowds babbled up through the second floor window of the room where Jesus and the disciples were sharing the evening meal together. The street noise made it hard to hear Jesus' soft instruction to Judas, "Hurry and do what you must."

The eleven disciples saw Judas suddenly leave the room. He hadn't even eaten. They had no idea that he was going to betray Jesus.

But Jesus knew where Judas was going. He stared for a little while at the open doorway through which Judas had just walked. The disciples waited to hear what he would say.

Jesus took a deep breath and sighed. Then, looking up at them, he answered their questioning eyes: "Now is the Son of Man glorified, and God is glorified in him."

The questioning faces remained blank. Jesus went on: "If God has been glorified in him, God will, in turn, glorify him in himself, and will glorify him soon."

"What do you mean?" Peter asked.

"My children," Jesus said, his eyes softening, "I am not to be with you much longer."

At this they all began to talk at once and combined with the noise from the street the room was a din of confusion.

Jesus raised his hand, seeking their silence. A hush fell within the room and the disciples waited for him to speak.. Even the noise from outside had momentarily stopped.

"I give you a new commandment," Jesus said. "Love one another." Some of the disciples began to look questioningly at each other.

Philip's hands popped open, seeking more, "But we do love one another," he exclaimed.

Jesus shook his head: "Such as my love has been for you, so must your love be for each other. This is how all will know you for my disciples: by your love for one

another." Jesus searched each of their faces and smiled lovingly upon them. It would be for the last time.

Not far away Judas was opening his hand to receive his bribe. Several Roman soldiers and temple guards were being summoned to receive their assignment to follow Judas out of the city and down into the Kidron Valley to the garden of Gethsemane.

✟

Jesus gave us the great commandment: to love one another as he loves us. If we can begin to get that one right, everything else will fall into place. Then the world will truly "know we are Christians by our love."

Sixth Sunday of Easter
John 14: 23-29

Final instructions

The meal was over and the disciples were finishing off the wine and listening to Jesus. He had been talking for a long time as if trying to remember everything and include it in what seemed to be final instructions.

Despite the warm wine in their stomachs the disciples all felt the growing tension in the room. Jesus was speaking with such urgency that the disciples began to know fear. They had not heard him speak like this before. The final instructions were coming fast.

One of the disciples raised his hand with a question. He was Thaddeus, the younger brother of James who was sometimes called Judas, but he was not Judas Iscariot who had already left the room to betray Jesus.

"Lord, how can it be that you will reveal yourself to us and not to the whole world?" he asked, wondering how a secret, private revelation could still be a glorious second coming of the Son of Man. Thaddeus had imagined there would be clouds of angels and trumpets sounding across the skies as Jesus returned in a blaze of light and splendor.

Jesus said to him, "Whoever loves me will obey my teaching. My Father will love him and my Father and I will come to him and live with him."

Thaddeus began to see that Jesus could only return to those who believed. He wondered how those who did not know Jesus could recognize him?

Jesus continued to explain: "Whoever does not love me does not obey my teaching. And the teaching you have heard is not mine, but comes from the Father who sent me."

James decided to help his younger brother. "You don't expect the Romans to know what we know, do you?"

Jesus sat upright and drank the last of his wine. Setting the cup back on the table, he looked across the room at young Thaddeus: "I have told you this while I am still with you. The helper, the Holy Spirit, whom the father will send in my name, will teach you everything and make you remember all that I have told you."

Thaddeus' face relaxed at this because he had been trying to remember it all and his head was already full of confusion.

Seeing a wave of peace crossing Thaddeus' face reminded Jesus to say: "Peace

is what I leave with you."

He paused, hoping they would all understand that they didn't have to do it alone and that he would be with them. "It is my own peace that I give you. I don't give it as the world does." Every face was now turned to him in rapt attention.

Jesus raised both hands as if to calm them: "Do not be worried or upset, don't be afraid. You heard me say 'I am leaving, but I will come back to you.'"

Jesus spoke to the disciples that night but his words have penetrated the hearts of all who listen. Through the centuries and the millennia he has come to live with each individual who has loved him. Many have sensed Jesus' presence in their lives by private experiences that can't really be put into words. He has already returned as he promised, coming to live with us if only we will open the doors of our hearts and invite him to come in.

Ascension of Our Lord
Luke 24: 46-53

Clothed with power
from on high

The Eleven Disciples stood on the mountain top staring up into the empty sky. A sudden gust of strong wind swirled around them, billowing their robes in a final caress. Where the image of Jesus had disappeared there was now only clouds floating in the summer blue sky.

Only a moment ago Jesus had been standing there before them, hands outstretched in a gesture of blessing. Then Jesus changed, becoming an image of transparent light, rising slowly above them. His love-filled eyes remained fixed on them as he rose higher and farther. Then he was no more. Only the sky remained.

Peter staggered back under the impossible assault on his senses. His eyes would not accept what they had just seen. His heart raced with the realization that Jesus was now gone. His ears were full with the sound of his own pounding heart. A giddy sense of joy began to fill him with a fireworks of wonderment. He had seen God with his own eyes. Shuddering with a sobbing laughter, Peter fell to the ground in adoration. The other disciples fell also, overwhelmed with the rapture.

Slowly they recovered and came to sitting positions there above the road to Bethany. Across the valley was Jerusalem where Jesus had told them to go and wait. Peter was astonished at the clarity of his thought. He could remember everything Jesus had said, but more, everything else was now making sense. The scriptures, the teachings, it was all so simple.

Jesus voice spoke inside Peter's memory: "See, I send down upon you the promise of my Father. Remain here in the city until you are clothed with power from on high."

Peter felt queasy as he climbed to his feet. It was mid-day and the thought of lunch raced across his mind, but quickly faded as the emotional impact of the experience overwhelmed him. Peter took a deep breath to recover and watched the others start to stand and brush themselves off.

Having shared the impossible vision, they found themselves unable to speak, moving silently together, bonded forever. They began to pray and, like a small flock of sheep, they huddled together in the rain of God's love.

They had been given the keys to the kingdom and it was now truly theirs to build. Jesus placed the challenge in their hands. Peter saw the others looking to him for instructions and heard himself saying to them, "We'd better get back to the city. Remember? He told us to remain there until we 'are clothed with power from on high.'"

On a distant hill a shepherd standing by his flock was looking down at the route of the Bethany road. He traced its winding route from the fortress gates of Jerusalem down into the Kidron Valley and then up the slope of the Mount of Olives. Squinting in the afternoon light, he saw an unusual column of men walking toward Jerusalem. Idly he counted them. There were eleven. The shepherd wondered what they were up to. "Probably nothing much," he said to his sheep.

✝

Many may respond to the Ascension of our Lord with the casual interest of the shepherd on the hillside. Many, like the Disciples, have the vision in their heart and are overwhelmed with God's love for us. For two thousand years the words that Jesus spoke that day have continued to be fulfilled through the Spirit which the Father sent. Believers are witnesses of this truth and have personally experienced the promise of the Father. Those who believe have been clothed with power from on high.

Pentecost Sunday
John 20: 19-23

The rain of Pentecost...

Peter's mind was like a raw sore filled with memories that wouldn't heal.

He could still see the bloody face of Jesus as he dragged his cross out of the city.

He could still feel the chill of the empty tomb where he and John found Jesus' blood-stained burial cloth folded there on the bench.

He could still see the shimmering light when Jesus appeared in the locked room. He could hear his living voice say "Peace be with you."

But strongest in his mind was the snap of the fiery streamer that had come down out of the sky and the roaring wind. Like a serpent dangling from a tree, the streamer of light stared Peter in the face. Then it struck, kissing him on the lips. "Pneuma!" Peter shouted in perfect Greek. Around the room he heard the foreigners speaking and understood their language. Terror overcame him.

Peter could take no more. He fled from the house, splashing out into the sudden rainstorm. He ran aimlessly through the narrow streets in search of the city gate. The harder he ran, the faster the memories chased him. Finally, wheezing with exhaustion Peter stumbled to a halt on the Kidron Road, just outside the city wall, and looked for a place to rest.

The rain stopped as suddenly as it had come, leaving a crispness on the cool air. The just-rinsed world smelled fresh and clean again. While the sun tried to find a way through the restless clouds overhead, Peter sat on a wet rock and gazed out over the Kidron Valley. Every few moments he would remember what had just happened and a shudder of emotion would ripple through him making him laugh and cry at the same time. It was a kiss from Jesus' spirit

The lofty dark walls of Jerusalem reared up behind Peter as if to drive him from the city. Beckoning from across the valley, Mount Tabor climbed up toward the Bethany Road which escaped to the east. In the valley below were the wet trees of the Garden of Gethsemane where Jesus had prayed to the Father before being taken by the authorities. Peter would pray there too.

His wet clothes were cold against his skin as Peter got up from the rock and started walking. Perhaps he would find some people with a warm campfire inside one of the caverns down in the Garden. He would tell them about Jesus as his clothes dried.

He would pray too, knowing that he could never be excused. He was forever commit-ted to keep following Jesus.

The first words of Jesus came back to Peter. "I will make you fishers of men." Peter smiled to himself as he realized telling Jesus' story was like going fishing.

"I can do that,'" he said aloud to himself.

Sunlight flashed between the parting clouds and spilled golden light on the rain-soaked road. The light made diamonds glitter on the rocks. Peter smiled as he felt the warmth on his back.

God chases us until we find him.

Most Holy Trinity
John 16: 12-15

The Trinity

The last light of the sunset streamed into the room, giving it a golden hue. As each of them finished their supper, the disciples made themselves comfortable. Jesus began to talk.

After a time, as if suddenly realizing something was wrong, Peter shifted from resting on his elbow to an upright sitting position. Jesus wasn't just having a normal after-dinner chat. This wasn't casual conversation. All of these things Jesus was saying and praying were his final words.

The sunset dissolved into a gray, dusky light which had become weaker than the flicker from the two lamps in the room. As he spoke, Jesus' voice was charged with emotion and his eyes glistened in the lamplight. Peter sensed the anguish that Jesus was enduring.

"I have much more to tell you, but you cannot bear it now," Jesus declared.

"I will bear it, Lord," Peter urged. "Tell us now! Who is coming? What does all this mean?"

Jesus lifted his gaze to Peter and continued. "When he comes, being the Spirit of Truth, he will guide you to all truth."

Peter and the other disciples looked at Jesus who was the only truth they knew. John's frown deepened. He spoke without looking up. "Why, Teacher, must someone else come and lead us to truth? Your truth is enough!"

Jesus turned to John and placed his hand on his shoulder. At Jesus' touch John looked up. His eyes glistened too.

"He will speak only what he hears and will announce to you the things to come," Jesus said. "In doing this he will give glory to me because he will have received from me what he will announce to you."

Peter tried to understand, but it was hard. He buried his face in his hands and massaged his temples. He reviewed the facts. Jesus was leaving. Jesus was sending a Spirit. The Spirit will only say what Jesus says. The Spirit will lead us to truth.

Peter asked. "Lord, I see you here before me. Yet you have said you and the Father are one. Now are you saying that you are also a Spirit that will come?"

Jesus replied, "All that the Father has belongs to me. That is why I said that what he will announce to you he will have from me."

Silence filled the room as each disciple pondered these words. The lamps flickered, causing their shadows to dance on the walls. Each man remained lost in his own thoughts. In a very short time the truth of the trinity would be unfolded before them.

✝

We affirm the Trinity that is celebrated this Sunday each time we cross ourselves, saying, "In the name of the Father, Son and Holy Spirit..." The Mass itself begins with a greeting which calls forth the grace of Jesus, love of God and fellowship of the Holy Spirit. The Trinity is the central mystery of our faith. We, like the disciples, must ponder this mystery, remaining lost in our own thoughts, until the Spirit comes and leads us to truth, just as Jesus foretold.

The Body and Blood of Christ
Luke 9: 11-17

The true food

Jesus leaned against the side of the boat and looked out across the lake. A faint breeze filled the sail and pushed the boat along the northern coast. They were too far offshore to hear their voices, but Jesus could see the great throngs of people following them by land, keeping pace with the boat.

Jesus was weary from the relentless crowds. Only on the lake was there respite. The hope of finding a lonely place to beach the boat looked brighter as the breeze freshened and the boat began to outdistance the people on shore.

Later they sailed into a quiet cove on the last gasps of the afternoon breeze. Climbing up the bank, Jesus and the disciples were astonished to find the people already there and waiting. There would be no quiet rest, even here.

Jesus waded through the patient and hopeful crowds, climbing halfway up the slope so that he could look back down on them and the deepening blue of the lake. Bethsaida was barely visible some miles to the west. Sunset would be upon them quickly.

When the five loaves and two fishes were presented to Jesus he remembered back to the day at Cana with his mother when the first miracle happened. He also saw forward to another breaking of the bread that would soon take place in Jerusalem. He then empowered the disciples to distribute the food. As they pulled the loaves in two, each half doubled its size.

✞

In the multiplication of the loaves we can see the foretelling of Jesus' last supper. In both instances the bread is blessed and broken and given to all to be shared. The miracle continues every time we celebrate Eucharist. Millions are fed.

Both stories also provide us with our own life challenge in the words Jesus spoke to the Twelve: "Why do you not give them something to eat yourselves?" We are called to feed one another! God empowers us to perform "miracles" in our time and place if we are willing to use the gifts of our own ministry. All we need to do is to say: "Yes, Lord."

The Sundays of Ordinary Time

Second Sunday in Ordinary Time
John 2, 1-12

Let there be wine!

The servants carefully filled each of the six stone jars. Jesus watched silently as they first poured from buckets and finished by ladling water until it reached the top.

Jesus studied the brimming jars and realized that clouds from the afternoon sky were reflected on the water's surface. He imagined entering the reflection and walking beneath those clouds in another time and place. He took a deep breath and sighed. As he inhaled again he felt a satisfying fullness of peace. Jesus seemed charged with the full power of God. Closing his eyes, he breathed a prayer. "Father, let this water become wine."

Instantly there was the taste of wine on his tongue and his nostrils were filled with the sharp scent of wine on the air. Jesus opened his eyes to see that the white clouds in the reflection were now brighter against the darker liquid in the jars. For a moment Jesus thought to dip his finger into the jar to taste the new wine, but he resisted. Filled with God's confidence, he had no need to test the results.

Stepping back from the jars, Jesus instructed the servants to go tell the chief wine steward that there was no longer a shortage of wine.

Jesus turned and faced his mother and the others standing by her in silence. Mary's eyes narrowed slightly, sending a warm thanks to her son. The corners of Jesus' mouth twitched in a brief smile back at her. Then he lowered his gaze and left the patio, walking past them.

Soon the chief steward was marveling at the taste of the new wine. Cups were filled and everyone celebrated.

Away from the crowd, Jesus took no joy in the moment. His heart was filled with a cold dread as he realized what he had truly begun. His journey was started now. There would be no turning back from the path that would soon enough lead him to agony, passion and death.

✝

This Gospel story of Jesus' first miracle presents us with an opportunity to reflect on the beginning of Jesus' ministry. This can lead us to remember the beginning of our own faith journey. Somewhere in each of our lives there is a "wedding at Cana" experience" that marks our coming to faith. Hidden in among the years is this little jewel of experience that we can rediscover and hold up to the light of our lives

Third Sunday in Ordinary Time
Luke 1: 1-4, 4: 14-21

Fulfilled!

"It's bright this morning," said the man on the path with Jesus. He held his hand up to shield his eyes.

Jesus nodded in agreement, looking to the top of the path where the glaring white wall of Nazareth's synagogue reflected the sun. The building's eastern wall was awash in the brilliant sunlight of the clear morning.

As they drew closer, Jesus and the man were joined by others hurrying to observe the Sabbath morning prayer. Jesus looked around him at the many familiar faces. He had been gone for a long time and was glad to be back in his home synagogue again.

But Jesus knew things would never be the same. He was returning from being baptized by John; from his time in the desert; from his powerful preaching in Galilee;, and most recently from his first public miracle in Cana.

When he stepped through the doorway, Jesus saw that the synagogue was nearly filled. He looked along the rows of benches that faced each other across the center sanctuary. There was a seat down near the eastern wall where the Holy Ark was located. Jesus walked toward the Ark with its polished wood cabinets and shelves which were open wide to reveal the Torah, the heavy scroll which contained the Five Books of Moses. Crossing the room, Jesus walked past the Amud, a raised prayer desk from which the scrolls were read. He took his seat and listened with the others as the cantor chanted the seven sections of the day's reading and sang the accompanying prayers. As the Torah was carried in procession back to the Ark they began to say the Eighteen Blessings.

When they finished, Jesus rose from his seat and walked to the center of the room and stepped up onto the Amud. The chazen, an officer of the synagogue, went to the Ark and selected one of the other scrolls from the shelf containing the books of the prophets of Israel. He carried the Scroll of Isaiah to Jesus.

Jesus began to unroll the book and found the passage he planned to read. In stirring words it gave Isaiah's promise of liberty, freedom, sight for the blind, good news for the poor and a year of favor to all. Jesus gave the scroll back to the chazen and returned to his seat. It was the custom to stand for the reading but the Jews sat for the homily that followed.

From his seat, Jesus let his voice fill the room: "Today, this scripture passage is fulfilled in your hearing."

His astonishing statement overwhelmed them. The prophecy which Jesus had just read to them had been written five hundred years earlier. And now that prophecy was fulfilled by Jesus who was sitting right there among them.

They did not know what to say.

Today the prophecy of Isaiah is 2500 years old and still Jesus comes to us this Sunday telling us in the Gospel that Isaiah's prophecy has been fulfilled in him. Like those who sat in the synagogue that morning, we must come to realize that it is true. Jesus brings these promises to his believers, his followers. He also empowers us to make these promises come true by our own actions and good works.

Fourth Sunday in Ordinary Time
Luke 4: 21-30

A Prophet in our midst...

Jesus felt hard hands pushing on his back, shoving him toward the door of the Synagogue. Angry voices echoed in the building as the crowd bellowed their protest against him.

The circle of men closed tighter about him as they emerged into the sunlight.

"The Cliffs, The Cliffs!" one of the men shouted. Everyone in Nazareth knew about The Cliffs. The Jewish custom of stoning a lawbreaker began with throwing the offender from a cliff and then lobbing big rocks down on top of the person's chest and head. Jesus felt a rush of fear rise up in him as the angry crowd continued to herd him up the steep path that led to the top of The Cliffs.

The Sabbath Service at the Nazareth Synagogue had begun in the usual way. Jesus read the Scripture Reading from one of the scrolls just as he had done at a previous Sabbath. He returned to his seat to begin the discussion of the reading. From where he sat Jesus reminded everyone: "Today, this Scripture passage is fulfilled in your hearing."

Jesus was implying that he was the Messiah, the Anointed one, the one sent from God, the one the prophets had foretold. This was too much for those who had watched him grow up and live among them for nearly 30 years.

"You make great claims, Jesus," one of them said. "But aren't you just Joseph's son? Don't you work down at his shop? Who do you think you are to claim such things?"

Jesus dismissed it with a wave of his hand, "No prophet gains acceptance in his home town."

Then he went on to remind them of how the Prophet Elijah bypassed all the widows of Israel and was only sent to one widow in distant Sidon. He told them how the Prophet Elisha cured only one of many lepers, and the leper he cured was not a Jew, but a foreigner. The implication was that despite their faithfulness, God's prophet would overlook the Jews of Nazareth.

Enraged that Jesus could say such things to them, they rose up against him to drive his blasphemy from them.

At the top of the cliff they began to edge Jesus toward the precipice. As the

crowd advanced, several of the men behind the mob were already looking for suitable rocks to throw. Jesus turned to face their anger. He took one step backwards, sensing that the edge of the cliff was only one more step away.

A cold memory flashed across Jesus' mind. He was standing on the highest point of the Jerusalem Temple. Satan was taunting him again: "If you are the Son of God, throw yourself down from here."

In that moment Jesus' face hardened with resolve and he walked straight through the crowd. No one tried to stop him. They gave way. One of the men who had just selected a melon-sized rock stood up to see Jesus walk past him. Jesus only glanced at the heavy rock and the man dropped it instantly.

☦

It is understandable that the Jews of Nazareth had difficulty accepting Jesus. He was just a man like them, working to survive, living among them. They could not recognize him as anything more.

We modern-day Christians also struggle to recognize Jesus in our midst. He comes disguised in many different ways. One clue to his presence is that he always seeks our compassion and love. Have you seen him today?

Fifth Sunday in Ordinary Time
Luke 5: 1-11

'Put out into deep water...'

The morning sunlight sparkled on the Sea of Galilee. Grassy slopes swept down around the town of Capernaum before plunging themselves into the lake. At the edge of the fishing boat cove a large crowd of people was pressing in around one man. As Jesus spoke, the crowd continued to grow, and he backed, ankle deep into the water. They formed a half-circle around him. The people of Capernaum continued to arrive, overflowing the banks in their eagerness to hear this powerful preacher with supernatural power. Jesus noticed the two boats moored at the water's edge. Simon was sitting in the nearest boat.

"Let me come aboard," Jesus asked him. "Sure," Simon Peter said, leaning over the side, offering his hand. Jesus waded into the deeper water and taking Simon Peter's hand, climbed in the boat. He had already been preaching a long time and was glad to take a seat in the boat. With his soaking robes clinging to his legs, Jesus resumed preaching the word of God.

Afterward the crowd began to disperse, thoughtfully returning to their homes and workshops. The fishermen from the two boats, who had been cleaning their nets, waded out. They piled the nets in the storage bin near the stern. Having already fished through the long pre-dawn hours they were eager to return home for some sleep.

"Put out into deep water and lower your nets for a catch," Jesus ordered them. The fishermen were too tired to react. They just looked at him in amazement.

Peter began to protest. "We've been at it all night and have caught nothing..." The urgent look on Jesus' face made Peter change his mind. "...but if you say so, I will lower the nets."

"We're going out," Peter called over to James and John in the other boat. The grumbling fishermen climbed in after their nets and began to slowly row to the deep water.

The sun and the rising breeze began to dry Jesus' robes as he stood, clinging to the mast. As they rowed, the waters beneath the boats darkened as a great school of fish began to form and follow.

✝

"Putting out into deep water" is an act of faith. It may not seem like the thing to do. We may be too tired or too busy to do what we are called to do. But Peter did

it anyway and the result was enough to bring him to his knees before the all-power-
ful Jesus.

By this Gospel today, Jesus calls us to put out into the deep waters of our
faith. It is only by moving in that direction that we can truly come to trust and know
this Jesus who is already aboard. By our own action we lower the nets for a catch.
At the end of our life's voyage, when we pull our nets in, we will discover that our
amazing catch is the gift of life everlasting.

Blessed are the poor...

To the west of Capernaum the hills pile on top of one another, rising more than 2,400 feet above the surface of the lake. Jesus and his Disciples were returning from this high country and were heading back down to the lake. Peter's home town of Capernaum was still more than a dozen miles away. From the crests of some of the higher hills they caught glimpses of the deep-blue Sea of Galilee sprawling in the distance beneath them.

Peter was in a foul mood, recalling the absence of his breakfast. "We never missed breakfast before," he growled to Jesus. "Even when our fishing nets were empty we always had plenty of food. We had money too! We could always buy something, anything! We were even going to buy another boat because our business was good. Now look at me. No boat, no business, no money, no breakfast!" Jesus smiled patiently and kept walking on the downslope trail.

Peter's anger continued to rise until it surpassed his hunger and finally left him hopeless and filled with remorse. He had abandoned everything and now he was as poor as the least of beggars.

"Even the beggars have something to eat," Peter blurted aloud for anyone to hear.

None of the others joined in Peter's protest. They knew that this angry morning should best be left alone. In another hour or so they would be reaching the eucalyptus grove on the plateau. There the crowds would already be assembled and there would be plenty of food and drink to share.

The morning wore on and by the time the sun was overhead the sweaty column of men reached a crest from which they could see the plateau and the tall trees. In the shade of the grove the large crowd was waiting for them. Jesus walked into their midst with the confident strides of a conqueror. The people cheered when Jesus reached them. They made him welcome, offering their places so that he and the Disciples could sit in the shade. Once seated, Peter was happy to see that cool water and food was being brought for all of them.

After the lunch was finished Jesus got up to preach. He first surveyed the large crowd seated under the trees. Many had come long distances to hear Jesus and they would not be disappointed.

Then raising his eyes to his Disciples, Jesus said: "Blest are you poor..."

The word "poor" caused Peter to look down, remembering his earlier complaints about being poor. When Peter looked up again he saw that Jesus had paused and was looking directly at him.

Jesus continued: "...the reign of God is yours. Blest are you who hunger; filled you shall be..."

Peter could not look up again. His eyes were full of tears.

✝

Like Peter, we all have struggled on our faith journey. When we "miss breakfast" it's hard to think about the great treasures that our Creator has in store for us. When things go wrong it is hard to realize that Jesus is at our side. Often we cannot sense him bearing us up on eagle's wings. But then we are given those joyous moments when we realize that the Beatitudes he preached that day are preached to us as well. We are blest, and our reward shall be great in heaven!.

In full measure...

Peter got up from where he had been sitting and walked away from the group. From the corner of his eye, Jesus saw the big fisherman leaving. Peter walked down the hill to a place where he could stand alone, looking out at the Sea of Galilee. The lines in his face were hard as he argued with himself.

He had seen Jesus perform miracles of healing and feeding and walking on water. He had himself hauled the burgeoning nets into his boat, nearly sinking it with a huge catch of fish. He had come to know that the man he followed was more than just a man. Because of this Peter had no choice but to continue to follow Jesus.

But now the stakes were getting higher. Jesus had just told him that to be a follower, a disciple, he would have to imitate God in mercy and forgiveness. This meant Peter would have to love his enemies, turn the other cheek, and give away both his robe and his tunic.

Peter could not imagine himself allowing someone to hit him. Just thinking about it made him flex his fists as a hot rage flared through him.

Feeling the breeze blowing in off the water reminded Peter of his boat and the years he had made his living out there on the sea. A part of him wished that he could go back to Capernaum, retrieve his boat and be free of Jesus and these impossible teachings.

"Peter, you can love your enemy and you can do good," Jesus said.

Startled, Peter turned to feel the warmth from the gentle smile on Jesus' face.

"I can't do this," he protested, throwing his hands into the air..

"Peter, if you only love those who love you, what good is that?"

He looked down at his feet and tried to imagine himself loving a man who had just hit him in the face. "How can I loan my earnings away and not expect to be repaid—and with interest! None of this makes sense."

Jesus continued: "Peter, be compassionate, as your Father is compassionate. Do not judge, and you will not be judged. Do not condemn, and you will not be condemned."

The two men stood in silence together, looking out at the lake below. The wind caressed their faces. Peter felt Jesus' hand on his shoulder. A peace seemed to flow from it. All the turmoil inside him subsided. He breathed deeply from the cool air and

turned again to look into the face of this strange man who had capsized his life.

Jesus said, "Give and it shall be given to you. Good measure pressed down, shaken together, running over, will they pour into the fold of your garment. For the measure you measure with will be measured back to you."

Like Peter, we come to know that to be a disciple we must become a new person. Christianity calls us to a conversion. It's easier not to change, so some may settle for a partial conversion where they wear only the words. They're easy to spot. We also can easily recognize the real disciples—those who not only talk the talk but walk the walk. Like Peter, we may struggle with the requirements of true discipleship, but it's already too late for us. We too must make full conversion in order to follow Jesus.

Eighth Sunday in Ordinary Time
Luke 6: 39-45

Remove the plank
in your own eye

The blind man lurched forward, flailing the air with his arms, falling into a display table filled with metal pots, bowls and pans. The clattering utensils spilled onto the smooth stone courtyard and rolled in all directions.

The astonished storekeeper scrambled to recover his wares as they went bouncing away like escaping prisoners.

Higher up, on the next level of the courtyards, Jesus was teaching his disciples. They sat facing each other in a circle. The commotion brought them to their feet and they hurried down the steps to help. Jesus and Peter were the first to reach the blind man. His groping hand clutched Jesus' arm as the two lifted him to his feet. Frightened and breathing hard, the blind man slowly regained his composure as Jesus and Peter carefully led him away from the clutter. The other disciples helped the merchant gather his utensils. Soon order was restored and the quiet morning continued.

After the excitement, seated again in the shady courtyard, Jesus used the event as a teaching example.

"Can a blind man act as a guide to a blind man?" Jesus asked. He didn't wait long for their answer before adding a second question: "Will they both not fall into a ditch?"

"A blind man could be the guide if he already knew the way," one of the disciples offered.

Jesus let the disciples consider the offered answer. His eyes seemed to ask them if they already knew the way.

Jesus went on to give them a new rule: "A student is not above his teacher, but every student when he has finished his studies will be on a par with his teacher."

The disciples pondered their present role as students and of Jesus as their teacher.

Jesus went on to open their eyes to the fact that we all can be blind to the truth—especially the truth about ourselves.

Jesus picked up a wooden table leg which some merchant must have left behind.

He whacked it against the palm of his hand and flashed a playful grin at his solemn students.

"Why look at the speck in your brother's eye when you miss the plank in your own?" Jesus asked.

Laying the wood aside, he told them to take the planks out of their own eyes first, "then you will see clearly enough to remove the speck from your brother's eye."

Jesus finished the morning lesson by leading the disciples out of the courtyard and down the lakefront road to stand beneath a fig tree. He snapped off one of the figs and held it up for them all to see. "A good tree does not produce decayed fruit any more than a decayed tree produces good fruit." Breaking the fig open he bit into the jelly interior. "Each tree is known by its yield."

The disciples began to understand that they would be known by what they did and what they produced in their lives.

✝

The valuable lessons of Jesus invite us to be good students, to see with new eyes, and to produce good fruit by our lives. It is a call to explore the scriptures and discover the Teacher anew. It is a challenge to see goodness and to be goodness. It is a mandate to love one another as the Teacher loves us.

'Lord, I am not worthy.'

Laurentius heard the knocking and opened his eyes to darkness.

"Enter," he ordered. One of his soldiers pushed the door open part of the way and gray, pre-dawn light spilled across the floor.

"I think Plinus is dying, sir," the young soldier announced.

"Alright," the centurion commander said, swinging his feet out of the bed. As he dressed Laurentius felt sickness churn in his stomach. Plinus had been in bed at the hospital tent for weeks. His condition had slowly been getting worse.

Laurentius remembered how for more than two decades Plinus had been his aide. They had served together in Rome, then Africa and now for these past 12 years here at the outpost camp in Galilee. In all that time Plinus had always been a respectful servant to his commander, but the years and their compatibility had softened the edges of their relationship. They'd become best friends.

The sun was just rising as the centurion commander entered the hospital tent and looked down on the gaunt figure of Plinus. He was lying on his side, shivering in fetal position. His breath came in labored rasps. Laurentius suddenly realized that Plinus was his only friend. . He squatted down and put his hand on his friend's shivering shoulder.

"What can I do sir?" the young soldier asked.

Laurentius rose to his feet, "Go down into Capernaum and bring the rabbis from the synagogue." The Roman Gods seemed to be doing nothing for Plinus. In his years at Capernaum Laurentius had come to know and respect the Jews and their faith in their one God. He had even let his soldiers help them when they were building their little temple building.

When the elders arrived they told Laurentius of the astonishing powers of this young Nazarean named Jesus. "We will go and ask him to come here," they said.

As they waited others from Capernaum came up to the Roman camp to give support to Laurentius and Plinus. They both had been good friends to the people and this was the least they could do.

When Jesus was seen approaching, Laurentius bent close to his friends from the town. "Go quickly, tell him: Lord, I am not worthy that you should enter my house…just say the word and my servant will be healed."

✝

The words of Laurentius, "Lord, I am not worthy," echo like an endless applause, spoken by millions of voices, across the centuries, over and over again. At every Eucharist we join in this declaration of humility and faith.

10th Sunday in Ordinary Time
Luke 7: 11-17

'I say to you, get up!'

Shahanna, the grief-stricken mother, led her only son's funeral procession as she painfully made her way up the street, her feet barely covered with cloth slippers. Shahanna's red eyes were wet with tears and she cried out in long, mournful wails. The sound rose from the depth of her heart and cut into the hearts of those behind her. The left side of her blouse was ripped just above her own heart as the traditional sign of mourning.

As a widow with no other children she wondered who would sit Shiva with her for the seven days of family mourning? Who would say Kaddish prayers each day? Now, how would she be able to survive alone?

Directly behind Shahanna, carried on a wooden pallet, was the dead body of her son, Mishakiel. Just two months ago he had stood at Shabbat service for his first aliya, and had read from the Torah. Yesterday he had taken a little food, but none for breakfast. Just hours ago he had tried to smile, but his illness had swept over him like an ocean wave, leaving him ashen and lifeless, still staring at the ceiling,

Following Mishakiel's funeral pallet was a large crowd of mourners. It appeared that almost everyone in the village of Nain had joined the cortege and was performing this deserving work of mercy.

Yesterday Jesus and his followers had walked most of the way from Capernaum. Last night they had camped in the fields. Today they passed the village cemetery on the northern outskirts of the town and were completing their easy, morning walk to Nain. Ahead Jesus saw the funeral procession coming and heard Shahanna's wailing. It went to his heart and he stopped walking, stepping aside to allow the mourners to pass.

Shahanna saw the group move aside and as she drew closer to them her eyes fixed on Jesus. His face was so intense and powerful that Shahanna stopped walking, locked motionless by his eyes.

"Do not cry," he said to her. Jesus stood alongside Mishakiel's litter and put his hand on the body. The mourners gasped. Touching the dead was the severest form of ritual uncleanliness.

"Young man," Jesus said with a powerful voice, "I say to you, get up!"

Mishakiel's eyes fluttered and color flowed back into his face. The young man

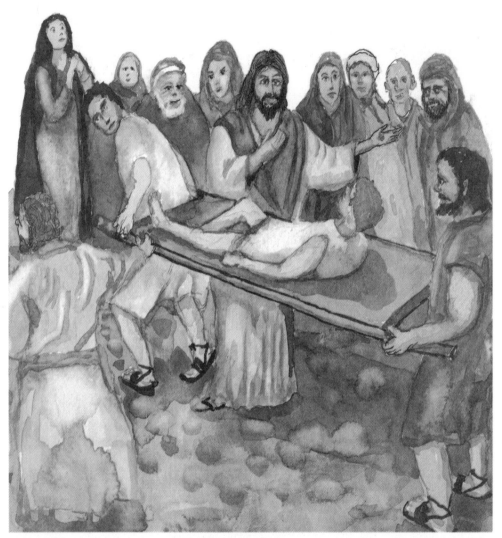

cleared his throat and sat upright. He blinked his eyes, wondering where he was. The mourners stood in astonished silence, looking at Mishakiel and then to the calm figure of Jesus who was gesturing for Shahanna to go to her reborn son.

Jesus has the power to bring us all back to life. It is his promise to those who believe.

11th Sunday in Ordinary Time
Luke 7: 36-8: 3

'Your sins are forgiven.'

Leah pulled the stopper from her bottle of perfume and poured the sweet oil onto Jesus' feet. The room was quickly filled with the pleasant aroma. The Pharisee, Simon, sniffed the air and looked disapprovingly at Leah, kneeling behind Jesus.

As Simon's dinner guest, Jesus was reclining on the low couch, propped up on one elbow. His feet hung over the edge of the couch and the woman, Leah, crying for her sins, was washing Jesus' feet with her tears. The scent of the oil and the presence of Jesus overwhelmed Leah and she began to cry all the more, bowing lower.

Simon watched as her wet tears sprinkled droplets onto Jesus' glossy feet. Offended by her presence in his house, Simon began to doubt that Jesus was a real prophet. If he were, he would know this sinful woman for what she was.

Jesus suddenly looked directly at Simon, startling him as if he had heard the things Simon was thinking..

"Simon, I have something to propose to you," Jesus said. The priest braced himself for what his "prophet" guest would say to him. Jesus told a story about gratitude in which a man with a large debt was told he did not have to repay it. Another man with only a small debt was forgiven too. Jesus asked Simon who would be more grateful, the man with the large debt or the one with the small debt. Simon agreed it would be the one with the large debt.

"See this woman?" Jesus asked, pointing to Leah who was gently drying Jesus' feet with her long black hair. "I came to your home and you provided me no water for my feet. She has washed my feet with her tears and wiped them with her hair. You gave me no kiss, but she has not ceased kissing my feet since I entered. You did not anoint my head with oil, but she has anointed my feet with perfume. I tell you that is why her many sins are forgiven—because of her great love."

Leah had backed away and was listening to Jesus' words of praise. She was no longer crying and hope was on her face. Jesus turned to her and said, "Your sins are forgiven. Your faith has been your salvation. Go now in peace."

☦

It may be difficult to imagine ourselves as the ones whose tears wash the feet of Jesus. Perhaps we perceive our sins as small and therefore we can't be expected

to be as grateful as the woman with great sins. As we grow richer in faith there is the even greater temptation for us to judge ourselves as worthy—maybe even too worthy to wash Jesus' feet. Our dry tear ducts may be the subtle sin. The story challenges us to get our perceptions straightened out. To know that every breath is a gift. To know that our little time of life is short and that we should make haste to pour out the perfume of our love on the feet of Jesus walking in our midst.

Luke 9: 18-24
12th Sunday in Ordinary Time

The road south...

Long red streamers floated from the flagpoles atop the towers on the walls of the northern city of Caesarea Philippi. The light breeze lifted the Roman streamers which proclaimed this place was ruled under the Tetrarchy of Philip. Guards on the parapets surveyed the road to the north. It was filled with travelers heading for Damascus through the scorched sands of Syria. To the east was Mount Hermon from which waters flowed south to Lake Huleh. From Caesarea it was a long 30 mile walk to the Sea of Galilee.

In a grove of trees along that south road Jesus prayed alone. He sat with hands folded in his lap, lost in prayer as he stared aimlessly at his dusty, sandaled feet. He knew he was beginning a final journey to Jerusalem. From now on the direction would only be south.

Despite all that he had tried to preach and teach Jesus wondered if anyone really understood. He also wondered what his closest followers really thought. Hearing the disciples approaching from behind him, Jesus turned and tossed them his question: "Who do the crowds say that I am?"

James Alphaesis said: "Some say you are John the Baptist."

Simon, the zealot, responded. "I've heard them say you are Elijah, or one of the prophets from long ago, come back to life."

Jesus face grew stern. "And who do YOU say that I am?" He asked them, looking each in the eye and ending with Peter who tried to avoid the question by looking down.

"What about you, who do you say that I am," Jesus repeated.

Peter looked up, his face full of resolve: "You are God's Messiah." he announced.

Jesus face brightened with Peter's declaration. It was a much-needed and reassuring affirmation. Jesus rose to his feet and took the first step south, leading his flock back toward Galilee.

As they walked along the way, Jesus said to the Disciples: "If you want to come with me you must take up your cross every day and follow me." He let them think about that for a while.

Jesus was thinking about the danger that awaited him in Jerusalem. To strength-

en and reassure them, Jesus added: "Whoever wants to save his own life will lose it, but whoever loses his life for my sake will save it."

Back in school there were lots of things we had to learn. A common question to the instructor was "Are these questions going to be on the test?"

Jesus asks us some difficult question today. They are definitely on the test!

Who do we say that Jesus is?

Do we really know him?

Is he at the center of our life?

A good test to whatever our answers may be is the next question he put to the disciples. Are we willing to take up our cross each day in order to follow him? Are we willing to lose our life for his sake in order to save our life?

13th Sunday in Ordinary Time
Luke 9: 51-62

Into Samaria

It was the first day of the trip from Galilee to Jerusalem. They had been walking most of the day and were nearing a Samaritan village. Jesus had sent two of the disciples on ahead to see about food and lodging for the night. It was going be nice to rest.

At the top of a rise in the road ahead Jesus saw a Samaritan youth bend down to pick up a rock. Taunting him, the young man hefted the rock, pretending that he might throw it at Jesus and his disciples. When they came closer he moved to the side of the road and glared as Jesus and his disciples passed by.

Travel through Samaria offered a shorter route to Jerusalem but there was a price to pay in this hostile place. The Samaritans were a people of mixed Gentile and Jewish ancestry. They practiced magic and were believed therefore to be demon-possessed and diabolical. Yet they also worshiped the God of Israel, claiming to be descendants of Jacob whose water well at the foot of Mt. Gerizim was a holy site for the Samaritan people.

The mainstream Jews had chosen Jerusalem as the holy city, the city of David. Pilgrims making their way to Jerusalem for the Passover celebration were often heckled.

The messengers were hurrying back to meet Jesus and the others on the road.

"These Samaritans won't let us enter their village," one of them snarled in anger. When he looked down the road behind them, the messenger noticed the youth who was still threatening the disciples with a rock. "Some of those up at the village have rocks too," he said.

"Then we will stay on the main road and further on we'll find another place to stop," Jesus announced.

"Do you want us to call fire down from heaven to destroy them?" James and John asked.

"No, we will leave them alone." Jesus ordered.

As they continued south, one of the group declared that he would follow Jesus wherever he went. The sun was setting and the prospect of sleeping by the road that night prompted Jesus to say "The foxes have lairs, the birds of the sky have nests, but the Son of Man has nowhere to lay his head."

As they continued, Jesus was walking next to a young man, a newcomer who had been curious about these travelers. Jesus invited him to really follow him.

"Let me bury my father first," he replied. In Jewish custom after a year the eldest son was responsible for reburying the dry bones of his father in a special box in a slot in the tomb wall. Yet Jesus demanded a violation of this commandment to honor father and mother.

"Let the dead bury their dead. Come away and proclaim the Kingdom of God," Jesus challenged.

When another who was invited to follow said he first wanted to say goodbye to his family, Jesus answered him "Whoever puts his hand to the plow but keeps looking back is unfit for the reign of God."

Jesus makes strict demands on those who would follow him. He teaches nonviolence. He teaches us to love our enemies. He places the kingdom and the reign of God above any earthly matters. He invites us to follow him into hostile lands, without food or water or a place to stay, without excuses, without looking back.

14th Sunday in Ordinary Time
Luke 10: 1-12, 17-20

The sending forth...

It was an impressive gathering. Nearly 100 men stood like an army, ready for battle. Peter and James and John and all the disciples encircled Jesus as he stepped up onto a stone ledge and raised his arms to quiet them. They all looked up, awaiting instructions.

Somehow Jesus had convinced all of these followers to go out and visit all the surrounding towns. Jesus had targeted 36 villages, asking them to go to each in teams of two. They would be reaching Gennesaret, Jotapata, Arbela, Tiberias, Cana, Beth she'arim and the cities to the north in Gentile territory.

The sting of rejection had already been felt by Jesus in Chorazin, a Gentile village only three miles north of Capernaum. There Jesus had been rejected by the people. The same had also occurred in Bethsaida another town in Gentile territory on the way to the Roman bastion at Philippi. And even in Capernaum there were those who would not open their ears to Jesus' preaching.

Jesus looked out at the eager faces remembering how the overwhelmed Moses had called forth God-fearing men to be his helpers. God said to Moses: "Assemble for me seventy of the elders of Israel...and I will take some of the spirit that is on you and bestow it on them that they may share the burden of the people with you."

It seemed in this moment that Scripture was being fulfilled all over again. Jesus' voice was charged with emotion as it rang out over the assembly: "Go! Be on your way. I am sending you like lambs in the midst of wolves." Jesus' outstretched his hands to shower his love down upon them.

His final instructions came rapid-fire: "Take no walking staff or traveling bag. Wear no sandals and greet no one along the way." He told them that when they are invited to stay at someone's home, to bless the house and those within it. He told them to eat and drink whatever they give to them. In this fellowship and hospitality they would find the kingdom. Then, most importantly, Jesus told the 72 missionaries to spread the news that "...the reign of God is at hand."

When Jesus finished preparing them he blessed them and gave them his peace and his power. Then he sent them out. They would learn in the days that followed that they had the awesome power of his name. They would be able to cast out demons and cure the sick.

✝

We are all asked to be Jesus' helpers. In this Gospel story we can find ourselves among the 72 being sent forth to the towns and villages of our time and place. Jesus has no hands but ours. This is our time to clothe ourselves in his power and go forth proclaiming "the reign of God is at hand."

15th Sunday in Ordinary Time
Luke 10: 25-37

Lessons in Discipleship

From the cool shade of the temple building the crowd watched the young lawyer stride confidently toward them. As he crossed the open courtyard, the sunlight brightened the colors of the expensive robes that flew about him. Reaching the shade, the lawyer's eyes narrowed searching out Jesus who was sitting among the others. One by one conversations stopped and everyone fell silent.

They already knew this man who had come to test Jesus. He had previously come to pose his questions. All were eager to hear the debate and the battle of wits that was sure to come.

Jesus nodded to the lawyer, inviting him to deliver his newest question.

"Rabbi," he said, honoring Jesus with the title, "what must I do to inherit everlasting life?" It was a common theological question among the Jews.

Jesus replied, "What is written in the law? How do you read it?"

His counter question neatly avoided any trap and invited the lawyer to demonstrate his own knowledge of the law. Jesus waited for the debater to explain his own opinion of what the law meant..

The young lawyer impressed everyone by quickly coming up with quotations which he knew from the scrolls of Deuteronomy and Leviticus: "You shall love the Lord your God with all your heart, with all your soul, with all your strength and with all your mind; and your neighbor as yourself."

Jesus praised him. "You have answered correctly. Do this and you shall live."

Not satisfied, the lawyer pressed on. "And who is my neighbor?"

Jesus began, telling a story about a man who was robbed and beaten. The first to find him was a priest who discovered him, bloodied and motionless by the roadside. Thinking him dead, the priest passed him by.

At this there was a murmur of talk from the crowd as they recalled that the priest could not risk defiling himself by touching the dead—even by letting his shadow fall upon the corpse.

"Likewise," Jesus continued, "there was a Levite..." The crowd joining in the juicy debate began to argue that even these Levite temple workers had to be cautious. The rules for them were less strict than for priests, but they too needed to avoid such defilement.

Jesus' story led them to next imagine the loathsome Samaritan coming upon the man who was beaten. This foreigner was full of compassion and helped the injured man in every way.

"Which of these three, in your opinion, was neighbor to the man who fell in with the robbers?" Jesus asked of the lawyer. The choice pitted the good and proper priest and Levite against the lowly and despised Samaritan man.

Not even wanting to say the word Samaritan, the lawyer submitted: "The one who showed compassion."

"Then go and do the same." Jesus said with authority.

✟

As "priests and Levites" have we walked by someone in need today? In our family are there those who have been "robbed and beaten" and left needing our help? In our parish community there are those who call out to us from the "road-side," seeking our help with the many projects and needs in our church. The world calls out to us as well. Most of us have mailboxes filled with invitations to be a good neighbor!

Did we help or did we "walk on by"? The young lawyer's original question was "What must I do to inherit everlasting life?" Clearly the answer is not to "walk on by" but rather to learn this valuable lesson in discipleship.

16th Sunday in Ordinary Time
Luke 10: 38-42

The right thing...

Like pale green coins the cucumber slices fell aside as Martha's knife furiously cut to the breadboard in steady whacks. The faster she cut, the angrier she became. There were still the tomatoes and no-one was watching the meat.

A peal of laughter came from the other room where Mary was sitting with Jesus. They were enjoying a glass of wine together. Martha suddenly remembered the bread and the pile of unwashed dishes from this morning.

The second round of laughter was all Martha could take. She stabbed her knife into a cucumber and stormed out into the living room.

Jesus was still laughing when he looked up at Martha's sudden entry. The laugh melted on his face as Martha fought back her tears: "Lord, don't you care that my sister has left me to do all the work by myself? Tell her to come and help me!"

Jesus glanced at Mary who was wide-eyed from Martha's outburst. He waited a moment before replying.

"Martha," he said softly, rising and going to her side. He gently put his arm around her. "Martha, you are worried and troubled over so many things." Her wet eyes looked up at Jesus. "Just one thing is really needed."

Martha wasn't yet ready for Jesus' teaching. She was still shaking with emotion. She knew that Mary wanted to be a disciple of Jesus. She also knew that Mary was fearless and wasn't afraid to step beyond the traditional boundaries assigned to women.

Jesus continued, "Mary has chosen the right thing and it will not be taken away from her."

Mary felt a flush of happiness course over her at these encouraging words from Jesus. She looked at him with thanks in her eyes. Then, without a word, she excused herself and went into the kitchen to help Martha with the preparations for the meal. Jesus went outside and rejoined the disciples who were eagerly awaiting the invitation to dinner.

✟

Martha's sister Mary is a model for all of us. Her example reminds us to take time to "smell the roses" and be with our Lord. If Jesus is living in our hearts, rid-

ing with us 24-hours a day, do we take time to say hello? We need to get out of the kitchen of "busy activity" and go sit at the feet of our "guest" and listen to him with all of our hearts.

17th Sunday in Ordinary Time
Luke 11: 1-13

Teach Us to Pray

The disciples waited at a respectful distance.

Jesus stood with his back to them. He was in prayer. The dark shade of the big tree draped over his shoulders like a thick shawl.

From the shade of another tree nearby, John sat with Andrew. John had his eyes fixed on Jesus who was deeply engaged in his prayer.

The closer they got to Jerusalem, the more Jesus seemed to be praying. John envied the way that Jesus could find such strength from his prayer.

"I wish I could pray like Jesus does," John said in a soft voice to Andrew.

"Don't you know your prayers?" Andrew asked.

"Sure, I've said them a lot. But Jesus prays differently—more strongly."

Just then Jesus opened his eyes and turned to walk back to the group.

John rose to meet him. "Lord," he said, "teach us to pray…"

Jesus looked at John, questioning him with his eyes.

John finished, "…to pray just as John the Baptizer taught his disciples to pray."

Jesus smiled, pleased at the request. "You don't need to say a lot of meaningless words like some of the pagans do," he began.

"What do we say?" John asked.

"Just pray, as we always do: 'Father, may your holy name be honored. Exalted and hallowed be your name."

John nodded, knowing well the standard Jewish prayer of honor to God. "We also honor his name by the way we live," John proudly added.

Jesus continued, "Then say, may your kingdom come." Jesus paused to let them think about that part.

After a moment Jesus continued with the personal petitions: "Give us this day our daily bread. Forgive us our sins; for we, too, forgive all who do us wrong." Jesus eyes wandered away from them when he said the next words: "…and subject us not to the trial."

John began to see that the prayer was an invitation to live more simply. "Just enough bread for today," John thought. "Pardon asked and pardon given. Hope and strength for life's journey." It was clear. John smiled at Jesus.

Jesus grinned back and then turned to walk up the hill a short distance. After a

few steps he turned back to them, waving them to join him. "Come with me, let me tell you a story,"

The men followed him up the slope to a spot where they all sat down on the grass.

✝

We have been receiving important lessons from Jesus these past few Sundays. Discipleship means helping others by being a good Samaritan. It means listening to Jesus, like Mary of Bethany. Now our discipleship is directed to persistent prayer. Just as we hunger for our daily bread, so must we also hunger for prayer to honor God and ask his blessing in our lives.

Abashol's Walk

Abashol looked out his window at his workers busy with goods from the newly arrived caravan. The warehouse was already so full he wondered how they would be able to pack it all in. The camels were led out leaving their burdens on the ground waiting to be unpacked and sorted.

'How much longer? How many more caravans?' Abashol asked himself. He was tired of buying and selling. Once proud of the numerous stalls he owned, Abashol no longer cared. With all his extra money he had invested in land and now had that to watch over. The leather bags he had hidden beneath the floor were heavy with coin.

A wave of depression stormed over him and Abashol realized he had become a slave to all this property and his possessions. He couldn't leave—even for a day. Caged in the cell of his own success, Abashol hungered for freedom.

"I'm going out," he told one of his clerks and moved out into the alleyway that led to the Beautiful Gate Road. It was rare that a man of Abashol's wealth would be seen walking alone on these roads.

He turned and headed toward the temple grounds and climbed the stairs onto Solomon's Portico. from higher up he could feel the breeze cool his face. There was a crowd gathered in the shade of the west wall. Abashol moved toward it. A young man was standing on a higher ledge waving his arms as he spoke. Abashol heard his voice, "...you have blessings in reserve for years to come. Relax! Eat heartily, drink well. Enjoy yourself."

The words were a perfect description of Abashol's life. He moved closer to hear more.

"But, God said to him," Jesus continued with his story, "'You fool! This very night your life shall be required of you. To whom will all this piled-up wealth of yours go?'"

The question went straight to Abashol's heart, piercing it like a sword's thrust. In the space of a few sentences Abashol's life was about to change forever.

Jesus continued: "That is the way it works with the man who grows rich for himself instead of growing rich in the sight of God."

Red-faced, Abashol pushed his way through the crowd to be able look into the young face of the man who possessed such simple wisdom. Jesus had finished his

story and was preparing to leave. He almost bumped into Abashol who was standing, breathlessly before him. Their eyes met and Jesus seemed to understand Abashol's anguish..

"How does one grow rich in the sight of God?" Abashol asked. Jesus put his hand on the rich man's back and began to explain.

✞

We don't have to be millionaires to understand this teaching and its message for our lives. The dollar amount is not important. Our worldly wealth and posses-sions take many forms. None of these forms accompany us into New Life.

Abashol went for a walk and wandered into the presence of Jesus' and heard his great teaching. Maybe we should also take a walk and wander into the presence of Jesus. There we can begin to re-learn this crucial lesson for ourselves.

Nineteenth Sunday of Ordinary Time
Luke 12: 32-48

Wherever your treasure lies...

A twig popped somewhere in the orange embers of the campfire. For a moment the yellow flames licked up as if trying to escape from the molten sea of coals. Jesus turned his skewered fish to cook the other side. All of the disciples were already wolfing down their meal, finishing off all of the bread except for one last piece which they had left for Jesus.

While his fish cooked, Jesus stood up to speak. A few stars were already lighting up in the pale sky as the last moments of day descended over the little group camped at the water's edge. Still chewing, Peter's beard danced in the lavender light as he looked up to hear what Jesus would say.

"Do not live in fear, little flock," Jesus said, knowing that his words would be hard for them to follow after the tribulations began. Peter chewed faster and smiled at the other men, as if to boast of his own personal bravery.

"It has pleased the Father to give you the kingdom," Jesus declared, urging them to realize how blessed they were with God's infinite spiritual riches. But Jesus knew how difficult it was going to be for them to separate their worldly riches from those promised from the Father.

Jesus stooped to check his fish. It needed to cook more. He continued, "Sell what you have and give to the poor." At this they all looked up, hoping he didn't really mean it. But he did.

"Get purses for yourselves that do not wear out," Jesus went on, "...a never-failing treasure with the Lord which no thief comes near nor any moth destroys."

James was listening intently. He swallowed his last bite of bread and asked Jesus. "But, Lord we need money here. How can we not have treasure here. What good is treasure in some other place?"

Jesus pointed at the sky to emphasize his teaching: "Wherever your treasure lies, there your heart will be."

✝

This Sunday Jesus invites us to think about the depth of our own faith. He tells us not to worry—the Father will give us everything. He says "sell what you have" and give yourselves to him. He says we have to choose between the treasures of the

world and the spiritual treasures of God. It should be a simple choice, but most of us seem to want both treasures. We're left with the hard question, "Where is your treasure, where is your true heart?"

To light a fire
upon the earth

It was the first time that 15-year old Yashim had ever been both alone and away overnight from his home in Capernaum. In the weeks before he had heard Jesus preach to the crowds in Capernaum. The words of Jesus had so inspired young Yashim that he decided to follow him. Earlier that day, when Jesus and the disciples left Capernaum, hiking south along the shore of the lake, Yashim had followed at a distance. Now night was falling and Yashim hungrily watched the group make camp and begin to cook their evening meal.

The disciples were circled around the small campfire warming their meal of fish and bread. Jesus noticed Yashim watching from a distance and called to the youth, "Are you hungry?"

Yashim was delighted when Jesus himself beckoned him to come and join them.

"Try this," Jesus said, offering Yashim a fish on a stick.

After the meal they all sat gazing into the last of the fire. Jesus broke their silence. "I have come to light a fire on the earth. How I wish the blaze were ignited!"

When some of the disciples began to look at him with questioning eyes, Jesus explained: "I have a baptism to receive. What anguish I feel until it is over."

He was talking about the trial ahead—a baptism of fire that would claim his life when they reached Jerusalem.

"Do you think I have come to establish peace on the earth? I assure you, the contrary is true; I have come for division."

Jesus looked over at young Yashim whose fervor to follow had divided him from his family this night. Jesus was speaking of division between those who believed in the kingdom which he foretold and those who were contented with things as they were. There would be no peace for those who wanted sameness—Jesus was bringing instead the sharp edge of newness.

People would have to choose which side they were on.

Jesus stared silently into the fire again. The dim orange light sketched his features on the black canvas of the night. Full of admiration, Yashim gazed at Jesus. He

knew that even though all of them would continue toward Jerusalem in the morning, he must return to his home in Capernaum. But he would be returning as a follower of Jesus. He would find the others who believed and together they would be new disciples, living out the teachings that Jesus had given to them.

Yashim chose to follow Jesus by becoming a disciple in his own community. Jesus said he wanted to ignite a fire of faith on this earth. As his followers, he wants us to ignite our fire of faith. He wants us to burn brightly for all to see. He wants us to light up the darkness in the places where we have been planted.

Twenty-first Sunday in Ordinary Time
Luke 13: 22-30

The Narrow Door

On their journey to Jerusalem, Jesus and the disciples had reached Archelais, a quiet country town in the region where the hills sloped down to the Jordan River.

Word of their arrival spread quickly through the region. Jesus and his followers first made their way to the town's public water well where they found several old men sitting on a stone bench. The name "Archelais" was chiseled into the rock seat. The disciple Philip looked at the inscription and showing off his knowledge announced: "Named in honor of one of King Herod's three sons."

The oldest of the men sitting on the bench stroked his white beard, got up, and ignoring Philip, approached Jesus. He looked closely into Jesus face and boasting his own knowledge declared: "And you are Jesus the teacher!"

Jesus smiled at him, "You say it."

The thirsty disciples waited for them to offer water from their well. A crowd was already gathering and Jesus began to talk about the kingdom and being saved from destruction.

Most Jews believed they would be saved in the time to come. Only a few isolated sects like the Essenes thought they were the only ones who would find God's favor.

The old man with the white beard raised a hand. "Sir, will just a few people be saved?"

Jesus didn't answer directly. He said, "Do your best to go in through the narrow door; because many people will surely try to go in but will not be able."

Some of the listeners who had been up to Jerusalem knew of the great gates to the city. When these gates were open, throngs could enter and one could even ride a camel beneath the high archways. But when the big, timbered doors were shut, only one person at a time could pass through the small, narrow door at the side.

The old man pondered this as Jesus went on to warn them that once the doors were shut, it would be too late.

Jesus then told them: "There will be wailing and grinding of teeth when you see Abraham, Isaac and Jacob, and all the prophets safe in the Kingdom of God, and you yourselves will be rejected."

The Jews assumed that God had prepared the Kingdom for Israel. They expected to participate in it with the prophets. Hearing Jesus' words made them consider that

Jesus himself was the narrow gate through which they might enter the Kingdom.

It was dusk and some of the disciples were being invited to stay in people's homes. Jesus was also invited, but he declined, wanting to find some time to pray alone. His return to Jerusalem was getting closer every day.

He would camp just outside the town. In the morning they would continue on to Jericho, only a morning's walk further south.

By moonrise Jesus had spread his robe on the ground and was sitting alone. He folded his hands together and lifted his eyes beyond the stars and began to pray.

✠

The narrow door is difficult to enter if you are overweight with self-indulgence and encumbered with lots of worldly baggage. In many ways, the narrow door is also the servant's entrance.

Narrow doors are for people who can leave it all behind and enter through it alone. Because it is a door, it can close. There will be a time when it will be too late for us. Today's Gospel urges us to hurry.

Our place

at the table...

J acob Ashrem was a wealthy man. He had a large vineyard, fields, flocks and even a little fishing enterprise in Capernaum. From the decorated courtyard of his large home Jacob and his guests commanded a sweeping view of his little kingdom.

The lake, sprawling below, was a deep blue today. Like thirsty soil, the lake absorbed the color from the crown of cloudless blue sky above its depths. Jacob's vineyards ambled in jagged rows down the slopes beneath his hilltop promontory. In the other direction, higher in the hills, Jacob's flocks of sheep were grazing.

Years of hard work were reflected in the craggy lines of Jacob's face which broke into a rare smile when he came up to Jesus. "Rabbi," he bellowed, showing big yellow teeth framed by his wiry, gray beard.

Immediately a servant appeared, offering cups of wine. Jacob took a cup from the tray and placed it in Jesus' hands.

"She's beautiful," Jesus said, glancing at Jacob's soon-to-be-married daughter. Jacob admired her too, then looking back at Jesus and his disciples, his voice was held captive with emotion. For a moment, Jacob was unable to speak and his eyes grew moist. Then his voice returned.

"Come, let's eat," he said, guiding Jesus toward the banquet inside. The rich smells of the roast lamb quickened their appetites as they stepped into the room. Already many of the guests had taken their places at the table. Looking up toward the head table, Jacob frowned and motioned for one of his servants to come. Some others were sitting at the table nearest the front where Jacob wanted Jesus and his disciples to have their place.

Jacob spoke privately to his servant and a few moments later the table was empty. Jacob himself took Jesus and his followers to their place. Soon the food began to arrive in heaping platters. From the head table Jacob and his daughter both nodded to Jesus who in turn raised his wine glass back to them.Then Jesus turned back to his disciples and began to teach them.

"When someone invites you to a wedding feast, do not sit down in the best place..." he began.

✝

The lesson Jesus teaches us is much more than proper etiquette. Jesus' invitation is to the great banquet in his kingdom. It is an invitation for those who are able to recognize their own lowliness—their own need for salvation. It's for those who know they don't deserve to attend. It is his gift. Jesus also challenges us to give our own feasts and banquets, not just for our friends and family but for others as well. We are asked to invite those who cannot repay us.

Twenty-Third Sunday of Ordinary Time
Luke 14: 25-33

Unless you
give up everything ...

T he people of the town of Tiberias had turned out in record numbers. There were so many that Jesus was forced to climb up onto a little lookout platform by the fishing harbor. With the lake as his dramatic backdrop, Jesus could be seen and heard by everyone.

He shouted to them, his clear words punching the ideas into place: "If anyone comes to me without turning his back on his father and mother, his wife and his children, his brothers and sisters, indeed his very self, he cannot be my follower." The harsh words were met by the troubled faces of those trying to understand.

Just beyond the crowd a group of six armed men marched up in pairs. They were soldiers of Herod Antipas, the Tetrarch of Galilee. The brisk cadence of their footfalls made Jesus stop for a moment to look down on them. They clattered to a halt and side-stepped into position, observing Jesus and the crowd. Their presence made it clear that people in high places were becoming concerned about the charisma and leadership of this Jesus.

The stone ledge platform upon which Jesus was standing was only five steps high. It looked like the beginning of a tower that had never been finished.

To make his point, Jesus paced around the platform, then throwing his arms out in invitation, he asked the crowd: "If one of you decides to build a tower, will he not first sit down and calculate the outlay to see if he has enough money to complete the project?"

He gave them a smile and then glanced down at the stones of his stubby little tower. The crowd roared with laughter and even the six soldiers lost their stern faces.

Jesus lifted his eyes, looking over the heads of the crowd to fix on the six soldiers at the back. Recalling Herod's recent military defeat at the hands of a rival king, he challenged: "Or if a king is about to march on another king to do battle with him, will he not sit down first and consider whether, with ten thousand men, he can withstand an enemy coming against him with twenty thousand? If he cannot, he will send a delegation while the enemy is still at a distance, asking for terms of peace. In the same way, none of you can be my disciple if he does not renounce all his possessions."

These were serious and disturbing words. They echoed in the minds of the crowd standing in respectful silence. Jesus decided it was enough preaching for today and slowly made his way down the platform's five steps. As he waded through the crowd Jesus felt their hands fall like a loving rain upon his back.

✟

Counting the cost is part of every decision. The cost of building towers and waging war are illustrations of the cost of following Jesus. The price of discipleship is not just our families but even ourselves. We must all consider the cost of discipleship and be willing to pay the price in full.

The kingdom is never "on sale." Yet, regardless of the cost, because God loves us so, it is always the greatest bargain in history.

Twenty-Fourth Sunday of Ordinary Time
Luke 15: 1-32

Precious in the sight of God

Abayam was face down in the dirt, snoring in the shade of the low rock wall alongside the Jericho road. His empty wineskin was evidence of the fuel he'd consumed for his drunken sleep. A fly wandered across his face causing Abayam to roll onto his back, belching up a blast of foul breath. He tried to moisten his lips but his tongue was too dry. Blinking helplessly into the light of a new day he propped himself up on one elbow and watched the blurry group of people walking by on the road. The man in the front of the group glanced down on Abayam and nodded to him.

Abayam's head swam in dizzy circles as he struggled to his feet and began to stagger back into town. Some women on the road made way for him as he lurched by in his filthy robes, reeking of sweat and urine. He felt for the pouch sewn inside his robe. There were still a few coins left from his last fishing pay. It was enough for another fuzzy day—a full wineskin as soon as Ben Asher's shutters were opened.

In the small park surrounding the town's water well, there were a dozen desolate men—some were regulars, others drifters. The two Jericho beggars had taken up their usual posts. The nervous-looking kid from Sidon was there again. His cold eyes narrowed as Abayam approached. Nearby were strangers, some armed, resting from their journeys.

Abayam gulped a drink of water and found a spot to wait. The water reactivated yesterday's wine making him feel nauseous. He held himself together and began to float into sleep, rocking gently on an imaginary lake.

Opening his eyes again Abayam realized a man in a very white robe had sat down next to him. He looked at him for a moment and Abayam recognized him as the guy he had seen on the road when he first woke up. It was the man who was entering town with a large group following behind him.

"Hello," Jesus said smiling expectantly at Abayam. "How are you feeling?"

In Abayam's next breath he felt something sparkle through his body. It was like the air was rinsing all his discomforts away. As this freshness seemed to flow through his entire body, Abayam's anxieties vanished. Suddenly happy, Abayam answered Jesus. "Great! I'm feeling just great!"

Jesus turned to the young kid from Sidon. "You seem to be a long way from home," he said, looking deep into the youth's narrow slit eyes.

"How do you know that?" the boy asked, his eyes opening wider.

"Just a hunch," Jesus smiled. "Just a hunch."

As Jesus engaged them in conversation he shared some figs with all of them. They began to eat together and the crowd began to grow. Some of Jericho's hated tax collectors even joined in.

"Don't tax these figs," Jesus joked, offering the sweet fruits to them.

From across the road a group of Pharisees were observing Jesus. Speaking in loud voices so that all could hear, they said to each other: "Look at this man Jesus. He welcomes outcasts and even eats with them."

Jesus responded by telling them a parable. "Suppose that one of you has a hundred sheep and loses one of them..." he began.

The story of the lost lamb, the lost coin and the prodigal son are all assurances that we each are precious in the sight of God. He lavishes this amazing world upon us and gives us our time in the sun. And regardless of who we are or what we do, he holds us gently in the palm of his hands.

Twenty-Fifth Sunday in Ordinary Time
Luke 16: 1-13

The best thief in Jerusalem

Jeptha was fast, probably the best thief in Jerusalem. In order to survive on the streets of the harsh city he had been forced to perfect his skills as a pickpocket.

From the little plaza across the street, Jesus saw Jeptha's quick hand dart into the traveling bag which hung from the shoulder of a well-dressed merchant. The man was so busy talking with two oil vendors he never felt Jeptha's lightning strike. Jesus saw the glint of metal as Jeptha pocketed his pickings.

Jesus sighed and leaned back against the high stone wall which shaded the little resting area where he and the disciples were spending the morning. Seeing the theft made Jesus focus on the ways of the world in which he lived.

Like a jungle, everyone seemed to be feeding on the next one. Jeptha stole from the merchant who was in the process of outwitting and stealing from his vendors. The vendors were stealing from the landowners and slave masters. The tax collectors were stealing from the treasuries of the kingdom and of Rome. It was like a busy hive of money-bees. Everyone taking a little here and a little there. It was a world where money was God.

Peter's beard was nestled on his chest and the big man's eyes were drooping. In another minute he would be sound asleep. Waking him with a rap on the leg, Jesus asked: "Remember the story I've told before about the rich man and his manager."

Peter swam up toward the surface of consciousness managed to spurt: "The rich man?"

"Yes," Jesus said, continuing to watch the passing scenes on the street.

"How did that go?" Peter asked.

Jesus retold the story of the man who was caught squandering the owner's money and was going to be fired for it, but who quickly took advantage of his final moments to reduce the debts owed to his employer and to get an immediate payment. He was probably only canceling the "cxtra" charges he had added for his own use. Hoping to get favors from the debtors in return, he instead was praised for his cleverness by the owner who kept him on.

"What I tell you is this:" Jesus said, "Make friends for yourselves through your use of this world's goods, so that when they fail you, a lasting reception will be yours."

Peter understood, seeing that Jesus was the only one who could offer a lasting reception in the world to come.

Jesus then turned to all the disciples and the others who were sitting there: "No servant can serve two masters...you cannot give yourself to God and to money."

This Gospel asks us to examine our own honesty and to identify our own true God. Can we be trusted in little things? Who is the master of our lives, money or God? What have we done with the wealth that has been given to us? It all leads to a sobering thought: What will we do on the day when money will fail and we must stand before God with only the actions of our lives as the evidence of our faithfulness?

Twenty-Sixth Sunday in Ordinary Time
Luke 16: 19-31

Once upon a time...

Wh   hen Maurus left the Roman garrison at Tiberius, he almost tripped over the little man. Crouched on his hands and knees, the beggar looked up at Maurus with pitiful eyes.

When he saw Maurus look back at him, the beggar quickly bobbed his head up and down as if he were crying out "Yes, yes!" With his few broken teeth, he tried to smile and lifted one cupped hand to receive a coin.

The well-fed Maurus looked down on the little man groveling at his feet. His deformity was hideous. He could not stand because only stumps protruded where his feet would have been.. His hungry eyes pleaded harder for a coin.

Maurus suddenly remembered the time and turned away. He hurried down the winding street toward his meeting with the Tiberias tax collectors. As he walked briskly through the town, Maurus' fat money pouch chafed against his chest. The bulging sack of coins hung beneath his tunic from a long leather cord around his neck. As he passed the Synagogue, Maurus glanced over at a big crowd gathered around a man who was standing at the top of the steps to the building. The man seemed to be looking directly at him.

"Once there was a rich man who dressed in purple and linen and feasted splendidly every day.," Jesus began in a loud voice. Maurus was wearing a purple tunic and thinking the speaker was making fun of him, he stopped and glared up at the man.

"At his gate lay a beggar named Lazarus who was covered with sores.." Jesus continued.

Maurus couldn't believe what he was hearing. How could the speaker have known about the beggar he had just nearly tripped over.

Jesus continued to tell his story about the beggar's death and the terrifying consequences—the rich man ending up in torment, begging for a taste of water from the former beggar.

Maurus fearfully recalled his own cold heartedness to the deformed beggar he'd just passed, vowing to give him a coin on his return.

As he hurried on to the meeting, the image of the beggar's broken toothed smile continued to haunt him. When Maurus returned to the Roman garrison later that day the beggar was nowhere to be found.

Everyday afterward he searched for the beggar. He never returned. Only the haunting memory of those pleading eyes remained.

Sometimes things just don't work out. We miss an opportunity and the consequences remain, unrelenting, unforgiving and unchangeable. Jesus' story reminds us of that and urges us to give our flowers to the living. Tomorrow may be too late. We move through life sandwiched between the past and the future. The only reality is the present moment which will never come again.

Hail Mary, full of grace!

Jesus was homesick. All day he felt the weight of a persistent melancholy. It followed him like a stray dog. During the evening meal his memories of Mary and Joseph filled his heart despite the annoying chatter of the disciples. Now, away from them and finally alone, Jesus went up into the hills. The grass was alive with the sound of insects. Their chirping reminded Jesus of a similar night in Nazareth, long ago.

Mary had finished cleaning up after their meal and had come outside to be with him. Mary seemed to always be busy working and this moment of rest was special. They stood together beneath the stars and the boy Jesus felt his mother's hand holding his. There were no words to break the silence as their eyes searched the crystal skies. A deep peace flowed into them and Mary's hand wriggled free to brush the hair away from Jesus face with her fingers. Mary was constant, always filled with faith. He turned to her and she hugged him close.   Jesus remembered the last time he had seen Mary when she was in the crowds by the lake. Someone recognized her and called out in praise: "How happy is the woman who bore you and nursed you."

Jesus had replied "Rather how happy are those who hear the word of God and obey it."

Jesus snapped himself back to the present, filling himself with the resolve of his own words to obey. It was hard to be out here, alone, on his own. He had no-one to hold him close and brush his hair away. There was only the thin strand of his faith and the huge presence of the difficult mission which he must obey.

Jesus followed the rising full moon back to the house where they were staying. He found the disciples sitting outside, splashed in moonlight and shadows from the trees. They were still talking about faith.

"Make our faith greater," one of them asked of Jesus.

"If you had faith as big as a mustard seed you could say to this sycamore tree, 'Pull yourself up by the roots and plant yourself in the sea!' and it would obey you."

Jesus went on: "Suppose one of you has a servant who is plowing or looking after the sheep. When he comes in from the field, do you tell him to hurry along and eat his meal? Of course not! Instead, you say to him, 'Get my supper ready, then put on your apron and wait on me while I eat and drink; after that you may have your meal.' The servant does not deserve thanks for obeying orders, does he."

The disciples grunted their agreement and a memory of Mary's constant working flashed through Jesus' mind.

Jesus finished: "It is the same with you; when you have done all you have been told to do, say "We are ordinary servants; we have only done our duty."

Jesus went to join the disciples, sitting on the ground and leaning back against one of the trees. His melancholy was fading and fresh strength was coming, borne on the realization that, like his mother, he himself was only a servant who was doing his expected duty.

☦

Mary is the servant, the handmaiden of the Lord, who answered God's call and did her expected duty. She is the first example of Christian faith. She abandoned her own self and said "Be it done unto me according to thy will."

She was an inspiration for Jesus. Hail Mary, full of grace. The Lord is indeed with you!

28th Sunday in Ordinary Time:
Luke 17: 11-19

Ten Lepers

The road south from Nazareth in Galilee took Jesus and his followers to the village of Nain. There in the morning shadow of the Hill of Morah Jesus was immediately recognized. Soon a great crowd gathered around him, remembering the great miracle he had performed there. They praised Jesus for raising a widow's son to life as he was being brought to burial.

Jesus declined their offer to stay and continued on the main road which led along the border of Samaria. By mid-day they were in sight of Mount Gilboa and were approaching a village where they planned to stop and rest. Peter saw a group of men coming toward them and asked Jesus: "How did they find out so fast?"

Jesus shrugged, wondering himself how word of their arrival had managed to precede them. As the villagers drew closer Jesus was able to see they were staggering and lurching, some of them bent over, wrapped in rags. They were lepers.

Because Jewish law quarantined lepers, they kept their distance. The ten men moved off the road, allowing Jesus to pass. They climbed higher on the hillside and positioned themselves there, beginning to call out: "Jesus, Master, have pity on us."

Looking up at them, even from the distance, Jesus could see their infirmities. One had great red blotches on his swollen face. Another was filled with scabs and clumps of hair were missing from his head. The law prescribed that once a skin disease was cured, the leper must present himself to one of the priests to be declared "clean" again. Until then, lepers were outcasts.

"Go, and let the priests examine you," Jesus declared. Joyful hope surged through all of them as they realized what Jesus' words meant. They ran on ahead to find the priest and on the way their skin cleared and they were restored.

One of the lepers, a man from Sebaste, in Samaria, noticed that his arms were no longer filled with scabs and sores. He stopped running and stared in amazement at his smooth arms and hands. He couldn't find the bald spots on his scalp and his fingers traced the smooth skin of his restored face. So suddenly freed from the dreaded disease, he was overcome with gratitude and turned to run back to Jesus. Some of the disciples began to back away when they saw him coming right at them.

"Praise God, praise God!" he shouted as he came, stumbling in his robe, to fall face down in front of Jesus. "Thank you Jesus. Thank you," he sobbed, looking up

through tear-filled eyes.

Jesus asked him, "There were ten of you. Where are the other nine?"

Turning to the disciples, he asked: "Why is this foreigner, a Samaritan, the only one who came back to give thanks to God?" No-one answered. Jesus looked down at the Samaritan at his feet. "Get up and go. Your faith has made you well," Jesus said. He got to his feet and Jesus placed his hand gently on the man's shoulder. They began to walk along together. The disciples fell in behind and they all continued toward the village.

✝

The lepers went out to find Jesus, hoping he would be able to end their hopeless situation. They asked him for a cure and they were rewarded for their faith.

The story invites us to do the same. We must go out and find Jesus in our lives. We must ask him for help, for a cure, for guidance. Whatever our petition, we must have both the faith and the strength to accept his response. And whatever his response, we must also give praise and thanks to him.

A lesson in prayer

Philip eyed his sizzling fish and rotated the skewer, giving the other side a few more minutes to cook. He picked his way back to the group, nearly stepping on Peter's outstretched hand. The day's journey had tired Peter out. When he lay back to rest his eyes, he had fallen fast asleep.

Most of the disciples were sitting in a circle around Jesus. He seemed to never tire, even now after the long walk. The day's goal had been to reach a camp at the edge of the River Jordan. Sore muscles and aching feet had brought many suggestions for an earlier and easier goal. But Jesus had held the disciples to it. They had reached the destination and Jesus was still full of energy, intently talking about prayer.

James stuck his scraped foot out in front of Jesus, "I prayed that we could have stopped at Beth Shan two hours ago."

"You prayed once." Jesus declared. "You must pray unceasingly. You must never become discouraged. You must be determined just as I was resolved to reach this camp today."

Philip suddenly remembered his fish and hurried back to the fire. James bent over his foot and carefully applied a small dab of oil to the red crease which had been cut by his sandal strap.

Jesus began to tell them a story about the judge who refused to hear a widow's complaint. This was strange because judges were supposed to fear God and defend the oppressed. Widows, who had no means of support, were often the most oppressed. The judge took sides with her creditor opponent. The widow persisted to such an extent that the judge finally gave in to her relentless determination and granted her request.

Andrew was back with his fish on a plate. He carefully picked around the bones and forked into the steaming white meat. He looked up, still chewing, and asked Jesus: "So the bad judge finally gave her justice?"

"Yes," Jesus said, "but how much more will God give you justice?"

"Even when we endure the sufferings the prophets predict at the end time?" Bartholemew asked, joining into the discussion.

"Yes," Jesus said, "if you do not fall away from the truth and if you pray with the same faith and fervor as did the widow in the story."

The smell of more fish cooking over the fire roused Peter and he lumbered to his feet. The big fisherman approached Matthew who was crouched by the fire, keeping an eye on his three fish. Peter smiled and raised his eyebrows in an invitation for Matthew to share his food.

"They're mine!" Matthew said, "Pray for your own,"

Peter looked hungrily over at Jesus and showed the group his empty hands. Everyone showed their empty hands and they all laughed.

"Okay, but just one," Matthew relented.

Peter grinned.

Jesus invites us to pray like the widow. From our unceasing prayer will come faith. This faith will then make us strong enough to carry our own cross when the time comes.

He who humbles himself...

It was nine in the morning and the Pharisee Aram hurried up the steps of the Great Temple. Even though he was a large man, heaped in great robes, he looked small as he passed between the towering pillars of Boaz and Jachin and entered the sanctuary. Aram sighed, drinking in the peaceful serenity of this holy place. It was good to be there close to God. To get even closer he climbed the additional steps that led to the entrance to the room of the holy of holies. There, looking down on those on the sanctuary level he began to pray his first prayers of the day. He would be back at noon and again at three and today would be even more special because it was the day before the Sabbath and he would fast from everything, including water.

Aram reflected on his goodness. Looking out at those praying in the sanctuary, he even felt a little sorry for them because they were all so filthy with sin. As Aram looked down he recognized Rabanius, a tax collector, huddled down on the floor in prayer. Aram snorted his contempt at the audacity of Rabanius to even come into the temple sanctuary.

Pleased with the perfection of his faithful worship, Aram bowed his head and fervently gave God his thanks: "I thank you God that I am not like the rest of men—grasping, crooked, adulterous—or even like this tax collector..."

From the cold stone of the sanctuary floor the tax collector Rabanius glanced up toward the room of the Holy of Holies. Standing near the entrance was a great Pharisee, head bowed in prayer. At such a sight of deep faith, Rabanius realized how unworthy he was. He pressed his face down onto the floor and softly beat his chest in remorse. He whispered his prayer slowly and softly: "O God, be merciful to me a sinner."

The sound of wings echoed high above as a dove flew from the topmost ledge of the temple walls, five stories above the sanctuary floor. It spiraled down sweeping close to Rabanius and then flapped through the entrance and disappeared in the bright morning light.

☫

How easy it is for us to become like the pious Pharisee. Our highly competitive culture teaches us to strive for excellence. Our human scorecard recognizes

only victories and achievements. Small wonder that we end up trying to get an A in our religion and faith class. Today's Gospel offers us a paradox—Jesus' words: "For everyone who exalts himself shall be humbled, while he who humbles himself shall be exalted."

31st Sunday in Ordinary Time
Luke 19: 1-10

'Hurry down, Zacchaeus!'

The woman appeared in the doorway and Zacchaeus frowned. He wasn't yet done with his breakfast, but he had much work to do, so taking the last of the bread he dabbed up the puddles of juice from the melon. "Clear it away," he commanded.

The morning sun sent fingers of light between the columns and into the room. Zacchaeus rose from the table and strolled outside to fill his lungs with the fresh air. He passed between the tall stone columns which made him look even shorter. Squinting up, Zacchaeus made note of another clear blue sky and its promise of a beautiful day. Inside at his desk Zacchaeus would be unable to enjoy it. The tax accountings were due to the Roman authorities and his report was far from complete.

Zacchaeus returned to his desk and stared sadly at the thick rolls of unfinished tax reports. He sighed and unrolled the first, dipping his pen into the ink.

By early afternoon the quiet of his study and the increasing warmth of the day began to lull Zacchaeus to sleep. His eyes closed and his head nodded forward.

From far away he heard the excited voice of his wife calling to him. Suddenly her voice was in his ear. "Zacchaeus," she shouted. "He's here. Jesus of Nazareth is passing through."

The tax collector swallowed hard and tried to pretend he had not been sleeping. "He's here?" Zacchaeus stammered thickly.

They both ran from the house and down the walkway to the road that led into the central district of Jericho. Zacchaeus quickly outdistanced his wife and soon could hear the noise of the crowds lining the Bethany Road. There were so many people crowding the road that little Zacchaeus couldn't see. He tried to squeeze in, but the townspeople smugly pressed themselves together to form an impenetrable wall for the hated little tax collector.

Zacchaeus growled and set out running far ahead of Jesus. Panting for air, he waited up ahead where the road passed under the shade of an old sycamore tree. Then a smirk flashed across Zacchaeus' face. He'd get the best spot of all! He shinnied up the trunk of the tree to the first branch and straddling it worked his way out to a center spot over the road. Looking back down the road, Zacchaeus was happy to see that Jesus and his followers were coming straight for him.

"He's so young," Zacchaeus thought as he watched the famous miracle worker

approach. When Jesus got closer he lifted his eyes toward the tree and saw Zacchaeus clinging there. A bolt of fear knifed into the tax collector as the eyes of Jesus locked with his own.

"Hurry down, Zacchaeus, because I must stay in your house today," Jesus said.

Zacchaeus reeled, almost losing his grip on the support branch. He held on hard, stunned by the realization that "He knows my name!"

✞

It is both fearsome and wondrous to realize that Jesus knows our name. Our creator, who has breathed us into life and filled us with his love, sets the meter for our heartbeats and walks with us through life. Yet, like Zacchaeus we are surprised that he knows our name, and even more, that as unworthy as we may think ourselves to be, he would choose to come to stay with us. It doesn't matter who we are when we realize whose we are. Knowing that we are God's child is then fearsome, for it calls us to real accountability for our lives.

32nd Sunday in Ordinary Time
Luke 20: 27-38

Whose wife shall she be?

Micha, the young stoneworker, had fallen backwards from the new wall. When his foot slipped he grasped at a newly-placed stone for balance. The stone had broken loose from the wall. Micha clutched the heavy stone all the way down. Landing on his back, the stone crushed his chest.

Everyone was still talking about this the next day. Among the priests and people surrounding Jesus on the steps of the Temple were several who had witnessed Micha's fall.

"He leaves a young widow with two children," one of them said.

"But his brother will take her and her children." another declared, relying on the Levirate laws from the Torah.

"And what if the next brother should fall from the wall?" a third one asked.

One of the Sadducees, well-versed in the books and the law, said, "Remember in the Book of Tobit the story of Sarah? She lost seven husbands, each killed in turn on his wedding night."

The idea germinated and another of the Sadducees decided to pose a question to Jesus. Since the Sadducees don't believe in any future resurrection of the bodies of the dead, this case would prove the point. After recounting the deaths of the seven subsequent brothers and finally the widow, he asked: "At the resurrection, whose wife will she be? Remember, seven married her."

It was a mocking question, posed to leave Jesus speechless. Everyone eagerly watched to see how Jesus would handle this situation.

After a short pause, Jesus spoke: "The children of this age marry and are given in marriage, but those judged worthy of a place in the age to come and of resurrection from the dead do not. They become like angels and are no longer liable to death. Sons of the resurrection, they are sons of God."

They marveled at his reply. Jesus went on to remind them of Moses and when he called the Lord the God of Abraham, Isaac and Jacob.

"God is not the God of the dead, but of the living. All are alive for him." Jesus concluded.

As they continued to talk among themselves, those there with Jesus, came to see

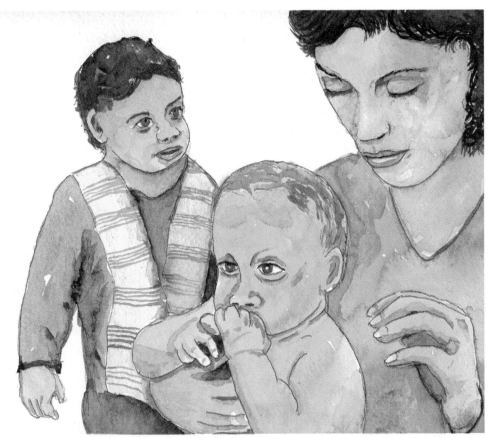

that the fullness of heavenly life leaves nothing more to desire. In the presence of God we are freed from the cares and pleasures of earthly life. We have become like the angels.

Today's Gospel story is one of the first proofs of our own resurrection. Our God is a God of the living, not of the dead. The story prepares us to understand the Resurrection of Jesus which is our absolute assurance that we too shall one day rise to the bright light of paradise.

33rd Sunday in Ordinary Time
Luke 21: 5-19

Patient endurance

They were Jewish authorities of some kind. The man with the black beard looked directly at Peter and seemed to recognize him. Speaking into the other's ear, he pointed at Peter. A bolt of fear coursed sharply through the fisherman's big chest as the image of Jesus under the Roman whip lashed through his mind. Peter ran.

As he lumbered through the streets of Jerusalem Peter tried to think of a place to hide. His leg muscles burned with pain but he couldn't stop or even take time to glance back and see if they were still following. Finally, gasping for air, Peter staggered up the stairs to hide in the upper room where he had spent his last evening with the Master. He yanked the door open and stumbled inside, holding the door shut against the light.

"Lock it," a voice behind him said. Gasping, Peter turned to dimly see several of Jesus' disciples sitting on the floor. Their faces were striped with prison bars of light coming through the closed slats of the window. "Sit with us, catch your breath."

Peter told how he knew they were looking for him. "They won't hesitate to kill all of you just as they killed Jesus," Peter warned.

They sat in the dim light and talked quietly. After a time it was clear that those chasing Peter were not going to find them. In louder voices they told each other their story of the fear that had overtaken them since Jesus was arrested. Then they began to remember.

"Only a few days ago," Peter began, "remember when Jesus told us that we would be manhandled and persecuted and put to trial before kings and governors? That's exactly what happened to him yesterday."

Andrew added, "Yes, and he spoke of signs in the sky like the lightening and the darkness yesterday."

James' voice was edged in fear, "The end of the world is upon us."

Peter scowled, trying to remember more of what Jesus had talked about. Only the fearful prediction that even family and friends would betray them, just as Judas had betrayed Jesus. For a moment Peter began to think of who among them might be the next Judas.

Matthew remembered the best part. "Yes, but I remember Jesus said that everyone would hate us because of him but not a hair on our head would be harmed. He

said that patient endurance would save our lives."

"It's hard to be patient when the authorities are looking for you," Peter growled. Patience was never one of his virtues, but endurance was. "We'll just have to stay out of sight," he said, resolving to wait in the room until it was dark.

The next morning Peter and the disciples would learn the miraculous news that Jesus was risen. Later in the week Jesus would appear to them in the upper room. As the disciples had walked at Jesus' side, now Jesus would walk at their side. With Jesus gift of the Holy Spirit, the first Christians would endure the rain of persecutions and their faith would flourish. Nothing has changed. With patient endurance we can endure the rain of our persecutions and our own faith will flourish.

Feast of Christ the King
Luke 23: 35-43

This day you shall be with me...

In the distance, somewhere beyond the pain, Jesus could hear the annoying rattle of dice. The cubes clattered across the flat rock and the centurions below him announced the numbers. The dice rolled again. "Six!" one of them shouted and he laughed jubilantly.

Jesus opened his eyes enough to see his robe being snatched up. The centurion folded it down tightly and stuffed it into his pack.

Jesus sank lower on the cross and the pain in his nailed arms exploded in ugly pulsing waves. Then he couldn't breathe and began to gasp for air. It was no use, there was no more delaying it, he would have to push up with his legs to free the pressure on his chest, balancing on the pain long enough to gulp a lungful of air. Desperately he pushed down against his nailed feet and stood on the piercing nail. The shock was a blinding white pain that overwhelmed him. Only the dark plateau of semi-consciousness gave him a place to hide.

Jesus opened his eyes again and helplessly looked out on the scene below him. His mother Mary's head was bowed. She was unable to stand any more of this horror and the sight of her there tore at Jesus' heart.

One of the centurions said to the winner of the robe, "You have a king's robe now." They chuckled, glancing up at the sign above Jesus head. "Let's give the king a little drink." He soaked a small sponge with some sour wine and balanced the dripping sponge on the point of his spear. He walked up to the cross and thrust the sponge up at Jesus mouth. He admired the endurance of this criminal. "Here, have some wine," he ordered. Jesus opened his eyes to see the sponge bobbing in front of him. "If you're the King of the Jews save yourself."

A man being crucified on the next cross heard the centurion's words. Snatching at this shred of hope, he shouted across to Jesus, "Aren't you the Messiah? Save yourself and us!"

Another, called Dismas, on the other side of Jesus, called back. "We both deserve our sentences but Jesus has done nothing wrong."

Painfully, Jesus rolled his head to his right to look at the man who had spoken.

Their eyes met for a knowing instant. Suddenly, the man cried with an anguished voice: "Jesus, remember me when you enter upon your reign."

"This day," Jesus rasped, looking up into the darkening sky, "you will be with me in paradise."

Jesus looked over at the other criminal and then back to his mother. Mary glanced up and Jesus lips twitched in a brief smile.

Like a helpless animal in the jaws of the predator, Jesus waited for darkness.

☩

Of course the Romans were wrong. Jesus was not the king of the Jews...he is king of all time, all places and all people. His triumph is that still today and for all tomorrows he can look over to us from his cross and because of it say, as he did to Dismas, "This day you shall be with me in paradise."

The Gospel Stories of Jesus for year C is available on a CD Rom

To facilitate the insertion of each weekly Gospel story into your church Sunday bulletin, or other program, this book has been downloaded onto a CD.

The text is in Microsoft Word and the accompanying illustration is stored as a black and white jpeg. This will enable you to flow the text into your particular format. You can size the illustration to fit your space.

Insert the CD in your computer, scroll to the current week and highlight the story. Then just copy and paste. The same procedure applies for the illustration.

Here's how to order the CD version:

To order by mail

Send your check for $9.95 to
The Gospel Stories of Jesus
32026 Trevor Avenue
Hayward, California 94544

To order by phone

call Deacon Dick Folger direct
at **510-475-7669**.

If you wish to order via the internet, just e-mail

dickfolger@aol.com
Please include the following information:
Your name, complete mailing address, credit card number and expiration date.
We will charge your credit card for $9.95 plus shipping and applicable sales tax.

Your postage paid order will be sent to you by U.S. Mail.